Rekindling the FLAME

PRINCIPALS

COMBATING

TEACHER

BURNOUT

BARBARA L. BROCK
MARILYN L. GRADY

CORWIN PRESS, INC.
A Sage Publications Company
Thousand Oaks, California

For information:

Corwin Press, Inc.
A Sage Publications Company
2455 Teller Road
Thousand Oaks, California 91320
E-mail: order@corwinpress.com

Sage Publications Ltd.
6 Bonhill Street
London EC2A 4PU
United Kingdom

Sage Publications India Pvt. Ltd.
M-32 Market
Greater Kailash I
New Delhi 110 048 India

Printed in the United States of America

Library of Congress Cataloging-in-Publication Data

Brock, Barbara L.
    Rekindling the flame: Principals combating teacher burnout/by
Barbara L. Brock, Marilyn L. Grady.
        p. cm.
Includes bibliographical references and index.
    ISBN 0-8039-6792-6 (cloth: alk. paper)
    ISBN 0-8039-6793-4 (pbk.: alk. paper)
    1. Teachers–Job stress.
    2. Burn out (Psychology)–Prevention.
    3. Teacher–principal relationships. I. Grady, Marilyn L. II. Title.
LB2840.2 .B76 2000
371.1′001′9–dc21   00–008165

This book is printed on acid-free paper.

00   01   02   03   04   05   10   9   8   7   6   5   4   3   2   1

Corwin Editorial Assistant:	Kylee Liegl
Production Editor:	Nevair Kabakian
Editorial Assistant:	Victoria Cheng
Designer:	Danielle Dillahunt
Typesetter:	Siva Math Setters, Chennai, India
Indexer:	Teri Greenberg
Cover Designer:	Oscar Desierto

Contents

Preface

Burnout is an increasingly serious and commonplace concern among educators. Teachers, once enthusiastic and dedicated, lose interest in their work, become cynical about students, and distance themselves from colleagues. They appear exhausted and overwhelmed. As the burnout process spirals downward, students become victims of poor teaching. Some teachers eventually leave the teaching profession. Other teachers, feeling that they have no alternatives, continue teaching with diminished productivity.

Burnout results from a variety of sources and varies with individuals. Factors that exacerbate burnout include the school environment, the role of the teacher, difficulty with parents or students, personal issues, and criticism from society. The personality of some teachers may make them more susceptible to burnout than others.

One of the issues perpetuating burnout is a lack of understanding on the part of principals and teachers. Burnout has nothing to do with a teacher's lack of ability or desire to be a good teacher. In fact, most teachers experiencing burnout were those most dedicated and enthusiastic when they started teaching.

This book is a guide for professors and practitioners of school administration who are interested in developing strategies to prevent burnout and to revitalize teachers who are experiencing burnout. The book provides a description of the origins and symptoms of burnout and a personality profile of teachers most susceptible to burnout. In addition, organizational issues and administrative roles that contribute to burnout are identified, along with suggestions for improvements.

ACKNOWLEDGMENTS

Grateful acknowledgement is extended to Phyliss Hasse for her expertise and skill in preparing the final manuscript and to Yuan Kun Yao for his able assistance. We extend thanks to the teachers and principals who shared their experiences and insights with us. Finally, we thank Alex, Natasha, Justin, and Elizabeth Grady for their consistently good humor and Michael Brock for his unfailing support.

Corwin gratefully acknowledges the help of the following reviewers:

Frank Buck
Graham Elementary School
Talladega, AL

Harriet Gould
Raymond Central Elementary School
Valparaiso, NE

Sandy Harris
Stephen F. Austin State University
Nacogdoches, TX

Carol Spencer
Best Practice Design
Addison, VT

About the Authors

Barbara L. Brock, EdD, is Associate Professor and Chair of the Education Department at Creighton University, Omaha, Nebraska. Her research areas include the principalship, leadership succession, and teacher development. She is coauthor of the books *Principals in Transition: Tips for Surviving Succession* and *From First-Year to First-Rate: Principals Guiding Beginning Teachers* and has written for a number of journals, including *Journal of School Leadership, Connections, Eduational Considerations*, and *Clearinghouse*. She is a member of the Mid-Western Educational Research Association, the National Council of Professors of Educational Administration, Phi Delta Kappa, Kappa Delta Pi, and the Jesuit National Honor Society (Alpha Sigma Nu). She has been a teacher and administrator in K-12 schools as well as at the college level. She received a bachelor's degree in art education from Briar Cliff College, Sioux City, Iowa; a master's degree in education with a specialty in K-12 school administration from Creighton University; and a doctoral degree in administration, curriculum, and instruction from the University of Nebraska-Lincoln.

Marilyn L. Grady, PhD, is Professor of Educational Administration at the University of Nebraska-Lincoln. Her research areas include leadership, the principalship, and superintendent/board relations. She has written for a number of journals, including *Planning and Changing, The High School Journal, The Journal of School Leadership,* and *Research in Rural Education* and has more than 100 publications to her credit. Her editorial board service includes *Educational Administration Quarterly, The Rural Educator, The Journal of At-Risk Issues, The Journal of School Leadership, Advancing Women in Leadership On-Line Journal,* and *The Journal for a Just and Caring Education.*

She coordinates an annual conference on women in educational leadership that attracts national attendance and that is in its 14th year. She has served on the executive board of the National Council of Professors of Educational Administration, the Center for the Study of Small/Rural Schools, and Phi Delta Kappa Chapter 15 and is a member of the American Educational Research Association, the Horace Mann League, the International Academy of Educational Leaders, the Schoolmasters Club, the American Association of School Administrators, the National Rural Education Association, the National Council of Professors of Educational Administration, the Mid-Western Educational Research Association, and Phi Delta Kappa. She has been an administrator in K-12 schools as well as at the college and university level. She received her bachelor's degree in history from Saint Mary's College, Notre Dame, Indiana, and her doctoral degree in educational administration with a specialty in leadership from The Ohio State University.

Part I

THE BURNOUT SYNDROME

When the Flame Flickers

Recognizing Burnout

...her exhaustion exceeds the physical; it is a condition of the spirit ...her soul is a windblown topsoil, a spent strip-mine.

— S. F. Freedman

BURNOUT

Teachers begin their first teaching assignment filled with enthusiasm and energy, ready to invest the time and energy necessary for success. They find the work meaningful and gain a sense of accomplishment from interacting with students and watching them learn. Passionate about their work, they plan to make a positive difference in the lives of students.

Passionate and dedicated teachers are most at risk for burnout. When their zeal and hard work are not rewarded, disillusionment prevails. Enthusiasm is replaced by despair. Like Tinkerbell in *Peter Pan*, their light grows dimmer, and they spiral toward burnout. The burnout process is complete when energy turns to exhaustion, involvement changes to detachment, and the sense of accomplishment becomes one of self-doubt, cynicism, and bitterness.

Individuals experiencing early stages of burnout are usually only vaguely aware of an undefined feeling of distress. Teachers dread going to work, feel exhausted, become indifferent to students, are dissatisfied with work performance, and avoid social situations. As the feelings intensify, problems at work and problems at home seem increasingly overwhelming and insurmountable. Work performance suffers. Teachers feel incompetent and incapable, take days off from work, live for weekends and vacations, and look forward to retirement (Cedoline, 1982; Huberman, 1993; Maslach & Leiter, 1997).

The Syndrome

Burnout is not an event, but rather a process, a chronic syndrome that becomes progressively worse. Burnout should not be confused with occasional feelings of discouragement and unhappiness. Individuals with chronic burnout perceive a discrepancy between the effort exerted and the rewards received. This discrepancy creates feelings of inconsequentiality and ineffectiveness (Farber, 1991; Friedman, 1995).

The American psychiatrist Freidenberg coined the term *burnout* in 1974 to characterize the psychological state of persons involved in emotionally charged interactions with clients and patients in helping relationships. Three elements commonly present in the behaviors exhibited by teachers experiencing burnout include:

1. Emotional exhaustion exhibited when teachers perceive themselves as unable to give to students as they did earlier in their careers

2. Depersonalization exhibited in negative, cynical, and callous attitudes toward students, parents, or colleagues

3. Reduced personal accomplishment—teachers perceive that they are ineffective in helping students to learn and in fulfilling their school responsibilities (Byrne, 1992)

The Symptoms

A high school teacher described her colleagues' classic burnout symptoms:

The morale in my school is extremely low and dropping due to lack of administrative support. The faculty is pretty much burned out. They feel overwhelmed, fatigued, unappreciated, useless, and underpaid. They are uncreative, complaining, do as little as possible, don't try anything new, skip functions, come to work late, leave early, and take a lot of sick days. There's no laughter or joking around in our teachers' lounge; faculty members are disconnected from each other.

Toward the kids, the teachers are negative, irritable, impatient, frustrated, and angry. They have very low expectations, don't care about discipline, and have poor rapport. They blame someone or something else for their problems without acknowledging the real cause.

Many teachers say they are either sleeping more or experiencing insomnia. They show signs of poor nutrition and overeating. They hate to go to work. Many are requesting transfers to another school.

Teachers suffering burnout generally exhibit symptoms in five general areas: physical, intellectual, social, emotional, and spiritual (Cedoline, 1982; Farber, 1991; Maslach & Leiter, 1997). The symptoms of burnout are multifaceted, with blurred distinctions at their intersections. Symptoms described in each of the areas should not be considered as discrete factors, but collectively as interwoven and interrelated factors. Table 1 (see Resources) provides a summary of the symptoms that are described in the following sections.

Physical. Feelings of chronic exhaustion are typical of teachers suffering burnout. They are tired when they get up in the morning and often feel unable to face another person or tackle another project. Sleep patterns are disturbed; they either experience difficulty sleeping or sleep excessively. One teacher contrasted her response to burnout with that of a friend who taught in the same school and also suffered burnout:

I used to go to school early and stay late. But the second year, I didn't even care. I would come home and sleep an hour and go to bed at 8 at night and not be able to get up in the morning. My friend's experience was that she couldn't sleep. I slept all the time. She never slept. She would maybe get 2 hours at a time of sleep. We both gained a lot of weight.

I couldn't tell you how much I gained because I stopped getting on the scales. I suspect I have lost 25 pounds since I've left there. Previously I had gone to most activities and I didn't care to go back at night. I didn't see one basketball game in the five years I was there.

Physical symptoms, such as tense muscles and recurring physical ailments, often occur. Migraine headaches, gastrointestinal problems, and high blood pressure are among the more common afflictions. Mental disturbances such as anxiety and depression may also occur. Some individuals compound the problem by turning to alcohol and drugs to alleviate their stress (Maslach & Leiter, 1997).

Individuals under stress will be more likely to have minor accidents, such as bumping, tripping, or falling, as one teacher described:

Mine was an accident, but sometimes I just think mentally you get yourself in a place where you want to escape. So I had two months where I was leaving once a week to go to physical therapy because I had fallen down the steps of the school.

Intellectual. Intellectually, individuals experiencing burnout have problems making decisions. They have difficulty making a choice and may delay or vacillate in their decisions. Once a decision is made, taking responsibility for the consequences is difficult. A typical response is, "No matter what I do, it isn't right."

Individuals suffering burnout have difficulty processing what they perceive as an overwhelming amount of information. They are unable to focus on a single task because they are distracted by all of the competing issues. Some people appear preoccupied, dazed, or overwhelmed. Others are easily angered and resentful of their workload.

Social. Withdrawal from colleagues and students characterizes the behavior of burned-out teachers. Many teachers report that they feel too exhausted to engage in hobbies or to socialize with friends after work hours. One teacher reported finding consolation from a pet: "I isolated myself [from friends]. It was a lonely time. We got a dog and I walked him everyday… I had him on a leash and [I felt like] he was pulling these negative feelings out of me…and his tail would wag… he made me happy." Another teacher described her isolation:

> I became more isolated. I had always been outgoing at school, popped into other people's rooms… I could go days without having an adult interaction. I stayed in my room. Other people stayed in their rooms. I was used to every night at the end of the school day going to the faculty room and we'd sit around. It was very pleasant because we were all interested in education and we'd say I read this article and I'm working with this kid. It wasn't a typical gossipy place, it was just several people got together and we were very close.

With burnout, teachers are less likely to be sympathetic or to become involved in their students' problems. Instead, they behave in a callous, cynical, or indifferent manner, and they display a lower tolerance for classroom disruption. In contrast, some teachers transfer to their students the affection that they need at the moment, living more for that period with adolescents or their students than for time with other adults (Huberman, 1993). One teacher, frustrated with the school's administration and alienated from colleagues, found reinforcement from students: "My students loved me. Even though I felt I wasn't doing a good job, they gave me a lot of positive strokes."

When the teacher does communicate, it is usually to indulge in cynicism and caustic humor to release frustration. The teacher lashes out at colleagues and students and is contemptuous toward the administration or school district. Humor takes the form of malicious jokes with references to students, parents, colleagues, and administrators.

Once burnout problems begin, a chain reaction of effects is set in motion. Stress and fatigue result in lessened productivity and efficiency and a diminished capacity to handle problems. Teachers are less apt to prepare adequately for class, feel less committed, and are less effective in their teaching. One teacher said, "I felt horrible because I cared about my students and felt that I was letting them down." Feelings of inadequacy perpetuate the cycle, work performance suffers, absenteeism increases, and students' needs are unserved (Byrne, 1992; Maslach & Leiter, 1997).

Emotional. Initially teachers deny the existence of burnout. Later, the teacher may project blame onto someone or something else rather than identifying the source and attempting to address the issue. Paranoia becomes a problem when teachers doubt their own competence and become defensive, competitive, and territorial—safeguarding their jobs. Trust becomes distrust.

Teachers experiencing burnout attempt to cope with the continual stress of helping by becoming detached. To do so they dehumanize students, dealing with them in an analytical manner, with a minimum of emotions (Byrne, 1992; Cedoline, 1982). Teachers become inflexible, religiously following rules and procedures to create routine, sterile interactions. They build an "emotional wall" to isolate themselves from students, parents, and colleagues.

Self-blame and loss of self-esteem are common attributes of teacher burnout. Many teachers feel that they are to blame for their burnout, believing that they must not have "what it takes" to be a teacher.

Spiritual. For teachers overcome with burnout, life seems dismal. After a long period of frustration, work satisfaction and self-confidence are gone. Relationships with students, colleagues, and family have been damaged. Even personal and spiritual values may be shaken. One teacher described her despair: "My relationship with God changed. I found no peace. I had no prayer life, no spiritual life. It was a dark night of the soul."

With any hope of accomplishing their goals gone, teachers suffering burnout want relief from the source of the frustration, an escape—to a new school or retirement. In many cases, bitter, resentful teachers, feeling let down by the profession, quit teaching, leaving careers that were once a source of pride and personal identity (Maslach & Leiter, 1997).

Projected Incidence

The phenomenon of burnout is most prevalent about halfway through a teaching career, between the ages of 33 and 45, for individuals with between 7 and 12 years of experience. One reason may be that teachers in their 30s and 40s are involved in establishing families and have committed themselves to their profession and community. They are most vulnerable to self-doubts regarding the wisdom of their career choice. This age group may feel locked into their teaching careers—too old and possibly not prepared to change careers, yet too young to retire.

The prevalence of teacher burnout may be as high as 40% of teachers suffering some degree of burnout during their career, and possibly as high as 50%. There is no indication that a period of burnout diminishes long-term teaching skill or the desire to grow professionally. However, burnout clearly leaves a toll in its wake. Indicators later in teaching careers suggest that burnout leaves some traces and is possibly never overcome (Brock, 1999; Farber, 1982; Huberman, 1993).

A veteran teacher described her feelings after an administrative change resulted in her choice to leave the school.

I had been a respected [teacher in the school for many years]. I lived in this town a long time, my daughter gradu-ated from this school. This was my school. It was a put down not to have people [the administration] listen to me. I decided that I would not let this [experience] make me bit-ter… [but] I have a little bit of bitterness left. I had looked at life through rose-colored glasses, thought if you're positive, everything would work out. I realize now that just doing the right thing won't get you a reward.

Burnout and Rustout

There is a difference between teachers who become burned out and those who "rust out." Teachers at risk for burnout are the hard-working, passionate, master teachers who dedicate themselves to students and to the pursuit of teaching. They make learning enjoy-able for students. Their continued interest in their students and con-sistent professional growth are inspirational. Often their work becomes the focus of their lives and their identities. The factor that creates risk for burnout is the same factor that makes them good teachers—their passionate dedication to their work. When they are not rewarded or recognized for their extraordinary effort, disillu-sionment can lead to burnout.

The "rustouts" entered teaching initially because jobs were available, not because they had a burning desire to be teachers. Most of them put in their time, inspiring no one. Some of these teachers are competent, and a few may even become excellent teachers. In general, however, they are not candidates for burnout, because they did not have zeal for teaching in the first place (Truch, 1980).

Other individuals show evidence from the start that teaching is not a suitable fit. After years of time and financial expenditures, however, many teachers are reluctant to quit. Others fear uncertain job markets or face pressure from family members or financial circumstances (Reinhold, 1996).

Problem Denial and Blame

Burnout does not occur as a crisis. Instead it sneaks up in a slow and insidious manner, slowly draining the spirit from the individual. For most people, awareness of displeasure is gradual.

Teachers frequently do not recognize or want to admit that they are experiencing burnout. Burnout is trivialized as something that occurs to teachers who cannot handle teaching. Others, after years of teaching, grow out of the work they have done for years. They need a change. They have been gradually lulled into unhappy complacency. Some teachers react to burnout with denial, claiming "there is no problem." Others, sensing their growing inadequacy, blame themselves. Burnout may be mistakenly considered a "flaw" in a teacher's personality. One burnout victim explained, "I felt like I was being blamed [for my burnout]; eventually I felt like it must be my fault." Although personality traits such as an inability to manage time or a compelling need to be liked and appreciated are nuisances and can exacerbate burnout, they should not be considered the primary source. In a solid, positive environment, these traits can become tolerable nuisances rather than career-threatening ones (Reinhold, 1996).

SUMMARY

Burnout occurs when prolonged job-related stress results in the inability to function effectively in one's job. Energy turns to exhaustion, involvement changes to detachment, and the sense of accomplishment becomes one of self-doubt. Teachers suffering burnout appear overwhelmed, exhausted, cynical, irritable, and withdrawn. Stress and fatigue result in lessened productivity, diminished capacity to handle problems, and feelings of inadequacy. Work performance suffers, and students' needs are unserved. Some bitter and resentful teachers quit teaching.

Initially, burnout was considered a "flaw" in an individual's personality, and little attention was paid to issues in the workplace that contributed to the malady. With the increased incidence of burnout and attrition among teachers, attention is currently focused on structuring school environments to decrease the incidence of burnout.

Flame Extinguishers

Sources of Burnout

A flame deprived of oxygen quickly extinguishes.

BLAMING THE VICTIM

Burnout has traditionally been considered an exclusively individual problem, a flaw in a teacher's personality. We blame the victim: "If the teacher can't cut it, she should get out of teaching." This type of thinking avoids the possibility that teachers may be working in school environments that create burnout or that exacerbate their proclivity toward burnout. Each year talented teachers who may have been "saved" leave the profession.

Burnout should be addressed primarily as a workplace factor and only secondarily as an individual issue. Although some personalities may be more predisposed to burnout than others, principals can do little to change the individual personalities of their teachers. Understanding the organizational conditions that foster or create burnout will make it possible to create healthier school environments (Huberman, 1993; Maslach & Leiter, 1997).

Researchers attribute teacher burnout to three factors: organizational conditions, administrative leadership style, and personality characteristics of teachers. Each of these factors is relevant in understanding how and why burnout occurs.

ORGANIZATIONAL ISSUES

Work Overload

Teachers suffer work overload when they experience too many demands, too little time, and too few resources to accomplish the work. Although the quantity of work is most frequently considered, the quality of work can also be a factor. Qualitative work overload refers to work that is perceived as too difficult to accomplish satisfactorily (Byrne, 1992; Maslach & Leiter, 1997).

Jane is a 32-year-old wife, mother of four, and sixth-grade teacher. Mornings are hectic, getting her children to day care and school. Her husband's job requires frequent travel, so he is seldom home. Once a week she has a 7:30 a.m. faculty meeting that destroys her morning routine. Evenings are crowded with dinner, laundry, correcting papers, transporting her children to their events, and attending school functions. She can't remember the last time she had an evening to herself or went out with her husband.

Budget cuts eliminated her school's paraprofessionals, so she has little assistance with the 6 special needs students in her class of 28 sixth graders. Several students read below grade level, and she struggles to find time to work with them. Three of the students have behavioral problems, keeping the class in continual upheaval. Standardized test scores are considered indicators of good teaching, and she worries that her class's scores will be low. In addition, some parents have voiced concerns that their "gifted children" are not being challenged in her classroom. The principal offers little support when parents complain. Lately, Jane has been calling in sick a lot—just to get a break.

The typical workload of teachers is a demanding stream of class preparations, assignments to correct, school committees and events, and meetings with parents. The pace is unforgiving, unrelenting, with few breaks. Assistance from paraprofessionals, resource teachers, and counselors is often scarce. School meetings and paperwork often extend far beyond the school day.

The classroom itself is a stage of unfolding psychological dilemmas and dramas. The issues and problems of students commingle with academics, and all of these affect the learning environment and must be addressed by the teacher. Compounding the problem is the isolation in which teaching occurs. No other adult is available for consultation, advice, or assistance.

Classroom Climate

The interactions of teacher and students in the classroom create the classroom climate. Overall positive interactions create a climate that stimulates and reinforces the teacher's efforts. Continual discipline problems, apathy, low achievement, and verbal and physical abuse by students are factors that can contribute to negative attitudes and subsequent teacher burnout.

Managing disruptive behavior in the classroom is a primary source of teacher stress (Brock, 1999; Kijai & Totten, 1995). Two student behaviors contribute to teacher burnout. The first is student disrespect toward the teacher or other students. The second is inattentiveness, failing to study, and failing examinations.

School Safety

School safety is becoming a concern for teachers in both urban and suburban settings (Black-Branch & Lamont, 1997; Brock, Nelson, Grady, & Losh, 1998; Grady, Bendezu, & Brock, 1996; Grady, Krumm, & Losh, 1997).

Alice is one example of a caring teacher for whom the threat of violence has interfered with her teaching and her personal life.

Alice teaches in an urban alternative school where she reports drug deals and substance abuse occurring on the school campus and in the restrooms. Weapons have been found on students, gang activity is present, and students engage in sex in the restrooms. Violence toward teachers and between students occurs but is seldom reported to police. The incidence of violence toward teachers remains low, because teachers, afraid of student retaliation, seldom enforce disciplinary measures. Although the school provides some security, Alice reports that the guards are worthless, untrained, and apathetic.

With the threat of potential violence and few measures to protect her, Alice stays in her office when she isn't teaching and goes home immediately after her last class. She has few interactions with other teachers, who she reports as being burned out. Even away from the school she remains watchful and wary when she finds herself in a group of people in stores, restaurants, and meetings. Fearing that she too will become burned out, she is looking for another job.

A recent study, conducted in 1991–1992 by the National Center for Education Statistics, reported that 19% of the 1,350 public school teachers studied had been verbally abused by a student, 9% had been threatened with injury, and 2% had been physically attacked. Half of the teachers reported that they were limited in their ability to maintain discipline by the lack of alternative placement programs available for disruptive students (Mansfield, as cited in Lawrence, 1998).

A wide continuum of security measures exists. At one end of the continuum are districts that report having no security measures, and at the other end of the continuum are districts with extensive security measures and proactive programs to assist troubled youth (Brock et al., 1998; Grady et al., 1996; Grady et al., 1997).

Compounding the problem is the lack of adequate statistics to measure the actual extent of violence toward teachers. Research on school crime is incomplete because of a lack of criteria for identifying and recording school crime. Some districts fail to see the necessity of recording criminal incidents to the police. Until uniform criteria and measures are adopted, the full extent of school crime will not be known (Lawrence, 1998).

Teachers are unprepared to cope with school violence. Their teacher preparation did not include training in violence control. They feel vulnerable and unable to protect themselves and their students. When security measures are not taken to protect them and the administration is unwilling to address the issue, they become increasingly fearful. They are prime candidates for burnout.

Role Conflict

Sometimes work pressures and demands seem to conflict. Jane, a fictitious name for a teacher interviewed for this study, was concerned about producing quality teaching for her class of diverse learners. She faced pressures to simultaneously meet the needs of the nonreaders, the gifted, and the average students. She felt pressure from their parents and expectations from the principal to produce high standardized test scores. In addition, her principal was not supportive of her choice of discipline for one of the students. Jane struggled with the conflicting role expectations.

Role conflict emerges from the clash of two or more sets of pressures. Compliance with one pressure makes compliance with the other more difficult, even impossible. Examples of role conflict include the quantity and quality of work to be accomplished within a time frame, meeting the needs of individual students of diverse ability levels while meeting the demands of an entire class of students, and taking positive disciplinary action with students while coping with negative support from a principal (Byrne, 1992). Role conflict occurs when teachers are required to teach special education students mainstreamed into their classrooms without the benefit of training or assistance from a special education teacher. Frustration results when the teachers are unable to adequately meet all of the students' academic needs.

Autonomy and Decision Making

Everyone likes to have control over their work life and input into the decisions that affect them. Participation in the organizational decision-making process is a critical factor in maintaining teacher morale, motivation, self-esteem, and job satisfaction. Teachers who participate in decisions that directly concern them have less job burnout. Teachers like to make choices and to have input into the outcomes for which they will be accountable (Maslach & Leiter, 1997).

Tom, a fictitious name for a teacher interviewed for this study, and the noncoaching faculty of his school were denied input into school decisions.

Tom teaches in a high school where sports surpass academics in importance. An athletic director reigns supreme, and the noncoaching faculty have little voice in school policies and procedures. Directives are delivered top down—from board to superintendent to principal to teacher. The only faculty who have any input are the coaches.

Most of the faculty would like to see improvement in the curriculum and would like some voice in school decisions. However, not given that opportunity, they spend their time complaining. Negativity is at an all-time high in the school. As a result, Tom doesn't venture into the faculty lounge or cafeteria anymore. He is discouraged with the scant value given to his teaching efforts. He works hard, and nobody seems to care. The last time he failed a student athlete, the parents, athletic director, and principal all chewed him out. Exceptions were made, and the student was allowed to remain on the team. Tom feels that he is not valued in the school or in the community. If nobody else cares, why should he? The enthusiasm he once had for teaching is gone.

Sometimes policies have a "one-size-fits-all" approach that does not allow for teacher innovation. The response from teachers is a mechanical one. Close monitoring also has the same effect. Teachers feel constrained and inhibited from taking initiative. Teachers feel that such behavior is demeaning and that it tells them they are not capable or trustworthy (Maslach & Leiter, 1997).

Some research shows that teachers generally believe their life in the workplace is controlled by others—an external locus of control. For instance, public concern for school effectiveness has resulted in school adoption of data to measure school outcomes. The public has demanded increased data-driven accountability by the teachers (Friedman, 1991). Another example is the performance-based accreditation standards implemented in some states. Both public pressures for data-driven accountability and the imposition of standards produce a stress mediated by locus of control. Teachers feel that they have no voice in what data should be collected or in what the standards should be, yet teachers are being held accountable for the outcomes (Hips & Halpin, 1991).

Sometimes the school's goals are ambiguous and seemingly unattainable. Although clarity of organizational goals is a prerequisite for an efficient organization and high morale, the extent to which goals are perceived by teachers to be attainable is a critical factor. If the school's goals are high and clearly defined, but the teachers never have a chance to express their feelings toward achieving them, the stage is set for burnout. Teachers will feel that they must work hard, be closely supervised, be measured regularly by standardized tests, and be under pressure for students to score high on educational outcomes that seem elusive and difficult to achieve (Friedman, 1991).

Teachers want to be included in decisions that affect curriculum content and how it should be taught and measured. They feel insulted and demeaned when "others" make uninformed curriculum choices for the students they teach. The stress resulting from accountability measures in which they had no voice is a factor that leads to burnout.

Isolation

The physical isolation of teaching is a common problem. Even more destructive are school environments where conflict exists between teachers and administration. When teachers lose their positive connection with colleagues, reported by teachers as a rewarding aspect of teaching, another burnout factor is set in motion (Farber, 1982).

Fairness

Mutual respect among people who work together is fundamental to a community. Trust, openness, and respect are key elements in a fair workplace. A lack of fairness is evident when workloads are distributed unevenly and administrators show favoritism.

Lack of fairness shows disrespect for teachers and breaks down the sense of community in the school. When teachers feel that administrators lack fairness in distributing work and rewards, they respond with bitterness, competitiveness, and retaliation. Instead of generating cooperation and extra effort, the administrator is faced with teachers doing only the minimum. Absenteeism increases (Maslach & Leiter, 1997).

Conflicting Values

Eager to obtain a teaching position, most new teachers pay little attention to the congruence of their values with those reflected in the school's policies and administration. They just want a job. Fortunately, for most teachers, value conflicts do not become a problem. However, in some situations, the school's policies and procedures clash with the values of the teacher. When this happens, a serious mismatch between the teacher and the school occurs, one that could have been avoided by careful hiring practices.

In other cases, teachers are caught in a confusing incongruence between the school's stated mission, goals, and values and the daily operation and procedures. The incongruence is apparent when a discipline policy states, "We believe in treating students with respect," but the teacher perceives the disciplinary measures used as embarrassing and disrespectful to students. The case of one of the teachers interviewed for this study follows:

> Susan was a highly respected English teacher and faculty leader in Oakdale High School. She loved teaching and cared deeply for her students. Over the years she had led the efforts to raise the school's academic standards and was proud of the high ACT scores of the seniors. An increasing number of students were going to college.
>
> When the school's administration changed, the standards were lowered and college prep classes eliminated. The new administration felt that the majority of students were not college bound and that the focus on academics should be lowered. As Susan watched her classes being canceled and the ACT scores falling, she felt that she no longer fit into the mission of the school. This had been her life's work and her identity. Now her work wasn't valued. She felt betrayed, became depressed, and sank into a deep despair. For the first time in her life, she started calling in sick. Eventually she left the school. Although she was able to secure a new and much happier position, the feelings of bitterness remain.

Discrepancy Between Effort and Reward

Teachers work for both extrinsic and intrinsic rewards. Teachers anticipate that their jobs will provide a salary, prestige, status, collaboration with colleagues, and the satisfaction of doing their job.

Most teachers do not expect great financial wealth when they begin teaching, but they do expect to receive a wealth of intrinsic rewards and an adequate salary.

Unfortunately, the salaries of many teachers do not provide financial security. Low salaries contribute to feelings of low self-esteem. When teachers are not rewarded adequately, they feel that they and their work are devalued. Contributing to low self-esteem is the need to moonlight to supplement income (Tishler & Ernest, 1989). An inadequate salary is a common cause of teacher burnout and attrition.

Low self-esteem due to salaries may be more prevalent for teachers in nonpublic schools. Teachers in a nonpublic school study by Brock (1999) reported that there should be no disparity between public and nonpublic teacher salaries. According to one teacher:

> All teachers should receive the same salary based on experience and educational credits no matter where they teach. Right now it depends upon the economics. There should be a balance.

When low salary is compounded by a lack of intrinsic rewards, burnout is almost certain to occur. Many teachers have little choice but to seek other employment.

Personal Issues

Personal circumstances may be serious enough to cause decreased productivity at work. Illness, death of a loved one, divorce, relationship problems, chemical dependency, difficulties with children, and financial problems are examples. For some teachers, geographical separations from friends, colleagues, and family members increase the likelihood of emotional exhaustion and anxiety. These factors, present in any degree, produce mental states that increase the risk for burnout. Personal problems, added to a new or difficult work situation, may produce the capstone event that makes work impossible (Huberman, 1993; Kijai & Totten, 1995).

Burnout frequently cannot be isolated to a single cause. The source of the burnout may occur at the intersection of personal life and work life. An example based on teacher interviews follows:

After 10 years of marriage, Marsha is going through a divorce. She is fighting with her husband for custody of her three children and is plagued with financial problems due to the divorce.

At school she is struggling with serious classroom discipline problems, uncooperative parents, and an unsupportive principal. She would like to quit teaching, but she feels trapped. She needs the income and is afraid to seek other employment. As she said, "This is all I know how to do. Where can I go? What can I do?"

The precise source of Marsha's burnout is complicated. What is certain, however, is that she has reached the limit of her ability to withstand stress and is suffering from burnout.

Nonpublic Schools

Church-related schools have unique stresses. Often teachers have multiple church-related responsibilities beyond the teaching function. For instance, some elementary teachers in Catholic schools are responsible for preparing children for sacraments, teaching religion, and preparing religious services with students. These duties are in addition to class preparations, yet they are considered very important components of the job. The additional burden may produce stress (Brock, 1999; Kijai & Totten, 1995).

In some nonpublic schools, parents and boards of education are influential in the selection and retention of teachers and administrators. Teachers perceive that their job security is dependent upon creating positive perceptions among parents of their students. In other cases, parental pressure may threaten the principal's job security and result in lack of support for teachers. An example based on teacher interviews follows:

Parents of the students at the private school in which John teaches seem to be more "in charge" of the school than the principal. John is tired of having the principal take the side of the parents whenever he tries to discipline a student for poor behavior in his classroom. Although the school's discipline policy is clear, most of the parents do not seem to think it applies to their child, and the principal sides with the parents.

The principal seems more concerned with keeping parents happy than running an orderly school. One thing John is sure of—he cannot count on the principal to support him.

ADMINISTRATIVE LEADERSHIP STYLE

During teacher training, teachers are prepared to work with a variety of individuals, including students, parents, colleagues, and principals. As a result, most teachers have interpersonal skills that enable them to adjust to varying styles of leadership. However, adjusting to a principal's leadership style and being satisfied with that style are two different issues. In fact, the interpersonal skill of the principal can be a factor in teacher job satisfaction.

Principal's Support

Social support by the principal and peers plays a major role in reducing job stress and subsequent burnout. Teachers who feel supported by their principal and peers are less likely to experience burnout.

When social support is not present, teachers feel that the principal is not on the "same side" as the teachers. The teachers believe that the principal's only interest is in protecting a personal image and position rather than in improving conditions for teachers or students. When the principal cannot be trusted for support, teachers learn not to "make waves" and not to create problems. A high school teacher reported, "Discipline in our school has gotten so bad, we don't bother trying to enforce the rules or send kids to the office because the principal won't support us. If parents complain, he takes their side…so what's the use."

Teachers dealing with demanding or dismissive parents depend on the principal to support their decisions. When principals fail to provide that support, a climate of distrust is created.

Chaotic Versus Micromanaged Schools

Teachers who work in a chaotic school environment or in a micromanaged school setting experience a lack of control over their work. When people feel out of control, burnout occurs. Thus, it is imperative for administrators to provide administrative leadership.

Schools without administrative leadership lack the direction and order that teaching requires. Principals who cannot or do not make decisions or who do not operate schools based on clear policies and procedures defeat the schools' purpose. Confusion reigns, students do not learn, and parents complain. Often discipline becomes a serious issue, and safety concerns develop for students and teachers. Teachers' morale declines as they struggle to teach in the midst of chaos. A teacher in an inner city alternative school said:

> The basis of the burnout in my school is poor administration. Yes, the kids are behavior problems, but the way they're treated is what fans the flames. They're mirroring the negative attitude of the teachers. The morale of the teachers is extremely low and dropping due to the lack of administrative support. We have no classroom observations, no staff development, and poor communication from the principal. We receive no support when students are sent to the office. When students skip classes and are tardy, the teachers don't bother reporting it anymore because there is no follow through when they do. For at least 2 out of 5 days, the principal disappears, just goes to lunch and doesn't come back. Personally, I think the principal is burned out himself.

Stifling Schools

In other instances, a school may be so well organized that it creates other pressures. When a school has a well-organized hierarchy, well-defined channels of communication, and a clearly defined set of policies and procedures, teachers feel pressured to conform to existing standards without having had a voice in defining them. Because communication occurs through a "chain of command," dialogue and discussion with the principal are precluded. This type of administrative structure confines teachers to well-defined roles and norms while stifling new ideas and a sense of community (Friedman, 1991).

Micromanaged Schools

In the most dismal cases, principals take control of every aspect of the school, leaving teachers feeling incompetent and untrustworthy. One teacher in a micromanaged school said she felt "like a peon in the king's manor." Another described the teachers as "acting like small children asking a parent for things." The following report of a visit to an elementary school describes a toxic school environment under the control of a principal whose response to a query about her management style was, "When I speak, everyone listens."

The school showed few indications of being inhabited by children. Stark white hallways, highly polished floors, and the lack of children's work displayed gave it an antiseptic appearance. A hush fell over the faculty room when the principal and I passed by. Only one student was spotted in the hall, and this student was promptly reprimanded.

Teachers reportedly lived in fear that the principal would visit and that they would not be adhering precisely to the time schedule for subjects. They worried that one of their students would be caught with candy or gum, meaning that teachers had failed their morning obligation to rid students of all sugar-laden contraband. Students weren't allowed to use the restroom unless the teacher called for a security guard to accompany them. Lesson plans were checked with regularity.

No congeniality existed among faculty. The principal had a few favorite teachers and openly criticized and ridiculed the rest. The faculty room was toxic with negativity. This was an extreme instance of micromanagement by a principal who had a need to control every aspect of the school.

PERSONALITY FACTORS

Some teachers' experiences lead them to view the demands of their job as threats, whereas others view the demands as challenges. Teachers who perceive a situation as challenging may be motivated to achieve, whereas teachers who perceive the same situation as stressful tend toward burnout (Friesen, Prokop, & Sarros, 1988).

The individual's perception of the importance of a situation determines how the person reacts to a perceived obstacle. Equal exposure to the same stimuli evokes different responses according to an individual's goals and beliefs. A teacher's level of dedication, perception of the importance of events, and ability to withstand the pressures of the job determine vulnerability to burnout (Farber, 1991; Friedman, 1995).

Anomie

Anomie, or a sense of meaninglessness about one's job, is a predicator of the depersonalization correlated with emotional exhaustion (Mazur & Lynch, 1989). Individuals experiencing anomie do not feel connected to other individuals, to an organization, or to a cause beyond themselves. They attempt to distance themselves from those individuals whom they perceive to be the source of their unhappiness. As a result, their attitudes are detached and callous, signaling the burnout stage of depersonalization.

Self-Concept

Self-concept is a major predictor of burnout. Individuals with low self-concept and little confidence are likely to become overburdened and emotionally depleted and thus vulnerable to burnout. Individuals with low self-concept assume a passive and deferential posture toward others, allowing themselves to be overwhelmed by the demands of the organization. Obstacles appear insurmountable. When such individuals subsequently fail in their efforts to overcome the obstacles, their low self-evaluations are reinforced.

Other research suggests that empathic self-esteem, or how one thinks that others think of one, is a predictor of burnout. Teachers who think that others have highly positive feelings about them may experience a greater degree of burnout. These teachers become emotionally exhausted trying to live up to others' expectations and standards (Mazur & Lynch, 1989).

Most individuals have a strong need for social approval. Events that are perceived as social rejection may be perceived as stressful.

Persons with low self-esteem are more threatened by rejection, and they are thus more vulnerable to stress and burnout.

Type A Personality

Another predictor of burnout is a personality, commonly referred to as type A, characterized by extremes of competitiveness, impatience, and desire for achievement. Individuals possessing the type A personality are compulsive overachievers who set unrealistic expectations for themselves and subsequently assume heavy work-loads. Teachers with type A personalities may be more susceptible to burnout.

Unrealistic Expectations

Teachers may enter the teaching profession with unrealistic expectations about what they can accomplish with students or within an institution. These highly idealistic and enthusiastic indi-viduals become disillusioned after multiple disappointments, often blaming themselves for what they perceive as personal failures. Understandably then, often the brightest and most dedicated teach-ers are those most likely to suffer. Teachers with the highest expec-tations, educational levels, and perceptions of competence are those most likely to suffer extreme disappointment and disillusionment when their expectations are not met (Townley, Thornburg, & Crompton, 1991).

Locus of Control

Another factor in burnout is teachers' external locus of control. Individuals who manifest an external locus of control perceive the causes and control of their problems as external to themselves, con-trolled by fate, luck, or other people. They are more likely to per-ceive obstacles as insurmountable than are individuals who have an internal locus of control and who see themselves as in charge of their life's events.

Teachers with an external locus of control have few coping strate-gies to deal constructively with challenges. Instead of taking con-structive action to solve their problems, they complain (Cadavit & Lunenburg, 1991).

Consider the reasons given by Jane, a junior high teacher, for receiving poor teaching evaluations: "I always get the worst classes—always the kids nobody else wants, the ones with poor attitudes and learning problems whose parents don't care if they study. Then the principal gives me poor evaluations, complaining that my students' test scores are poor. It isn't fair."

Jane perceives that her problem is created externally and that any possibility of controlling the problem is beyond her control. Instead of addressing the problem by finding a way to motivate her students, she complains. She is at a high risk for burnout because of her external locus of control.

Teachers who have an external locus of control are likely to have a custodial pupil control ideology, perceiving that students require firm discipline and direction from the teacher. Internally controlled teachers are more likely to perceive students in a positive manner, seeing them as disciplined, trustworthy, and responsible (Cadavit & Lunenburg, 1991).

SUMMARY

Burnout cannot be attributed to a single cause; rather, the cause is multifaceted and complex. Sources often emerge at the intersection of work, home, and personality factors. Blaming the victim is not a productive solution. Identifying burnout sources that occur in the workplace and that are within the control of the principal will prove to be a more productive option for principals, teachers, and students. Figure 1 (see Resources) represents factors in teacher burnout.

Smoldering Embers

The Cost of Burnout

Slight not what's near, while aiming at what's far.

—Euripides

BALANCE IS THE KEY

An old adage endures: "Hard work never hurt anyone." However, in the late 1980s, the Japanese discovered individuals suddenly dying from work overload, a syndrome that they called *Karoshi* (Reinhold, 1996). Clearly, under some conditions, work can be harmful to one's health.

Five different body systems are affected by reactions to work: the nervous system, the immune system, the endocrine system, the cardiovascular system, and the musculoskeletal system. When you are feeling anxious, angry, doubtful, or lonely because of events at work, the nervous system informs all of the other systems. The other systems mete out punishment in the form of illnesses ranging from mild to serious. Negative feelings such as failure, unhappiness, and discontentment decrease effectiveness and compromise your health.

The mind affects how you experience work and colors feelings you have about yourself. These reactions inform all body systems about how to behave when you are in a situation that does not fit or when the demands of your work seem overwhelming—when something disturbs your body's ecosystem (Reinhold, 1996).

Stress that results from working is not necessarily a negative. *Eustress*, or good stress, can be therapeutic and challenging. Stress that causes burnout has no redeeming features and serves only to escalate serious individual and organizational problems (Sarros & Sarros, 1990).

Work that generates "good stress" can be positive and actually enhance job performance. Doing your job well and being appreciated for what you do builds self-esteem and a sense of purpose. Job satisfaction can enhance the functioning of the cardiovascular and immune systems, increasing both health and longevity (Reinhold, 1996).

By contrast, when you do your job well and are not appreciated for what you do, self-esteem and sense of purpose are overcome by self-doubt and feelings of uselessness. Burnout is almost inevitable.

Burnout and the Workplace

Traditionally, burnout has been viewed as the problem of the individual. Teachers who experienced burnout were regarded as having personality flaws. They were encouraged to improve themselves. Workshops in stress reduction were provided as a solution. When improvement was not forthcoming, teachers were blamed, transferred to other schools, encouraged to retire, or terminated.

As a nation, we have recognized and focused considerable attention on safety hazards in the workplace while giving little attention to workplace conditions as they relate to overall job satisfaction and emotional well-being. School administrators now realize that, despite individual proclivity for burnout, attention to workplace conditions can increase teacher job satisfaction and well-being and decrease the potential for burnout (Reinhold, 1996).

THE PERSONAL PRICE

The personal price of burnout is great. Burnout erodes health and self-esteem. Relationships with family, friends, and colleagues are strained. Work performance dwindles, generating feelings of incompetence and creating a vicious cycle of despair. The very spirit of the individual is lost.

Health Issues

Physical symptoms that reveal a problem include chronic fatigue, insomnia, dizziness, nausea, allergies, breathing difficulties, skin problems, muscle aches and stiffness, menstrual difficulties, swollen glands, sore throat, recurrent flu, infections, colds, headaches, digestive problems, and back pain. Respiratory infections and headaches linger longer. Individuals may develop ulcers, high blood pressure, and other serious health problems (Maslach, 1982; Reinhold, 1996). One teacher described changes associated with burnout as follows:

> I called in sick often, which was a big change for me. Before, I seldom missed work. Now I didn't care. I was sick a lot, had a lot of back pains—I think I just wanted to avoid going to school.

Teachers may experience mental distress, such as depression and sleep disorders. As one teacher explained, "When I came home I took a nap, went to bed by 8 p.m., and still had difficulty getting up in the morning." Another teacher described her colleague: "She falls asleep at morning meetings." Teachers describe emotional exhaustion that is accompanied by physical exhaustion. They are tired and run down and have difficulty getting up in the morning to face each new day. They feel tense, wound up, and unable to relax. They experience insomnia, nightmares, sleepless nights of worry, and nagging, unnamed fears that something may go wrong.

People under pressure develop poor eating habits, skip meals, eat on the run, and use lunch to catch up on work. Individuals may eat compulsively or excessively, such as the teacher who complained, "I gained a lot of weight." Others eat less and experience weight loss.

Individuals under stress may cope with problems by turning to tranquilizers, drugs, and alcohol to unwind at the end of the day. These potentially habit-forming solutions have the potential for abuse. Erroneously perceived as a solution, they actually intensify the problem (Maslach, 1982; Maslach & Leiter, 1997).

Emotional Health

Psychological health is affected by burnout. Teachers may experience a sense of reduced personal accomplishment and a loss of self-esteem, as suggested by these teachers' comments.

I felt that I didn't belong anymore.
My identity had been my job and now it meant nothing.
On the outside it looked like I was doing OK, yet inwardly
   I wasn't.
I knew I wasn't doing a good job and blamed myself.

One teacher said, "Once I was so excited about teaching. Now all I do is yell at the kids. I feel so guilty, but I get so frustrated dealing with them all day, day after day." Feeling bad about oneself leads to even worse performance, which provides further evidence of one's lack of competence and thereby creates a self-fulfilling prophecy (Maslach, 1982).

Self-blame leads teachers to additional self-destructive behaviors. Teachers experiencing burnout often isolate themselves from others. They seclude themselves from the very people who might be able to help them. One teacher said, "I didn't go to the faculty room or cafeteria anymore. I didn't converse with other adults at school."

A breakdown in self-esteem is the result of an individual's sense of failure or a loss. With teachers, self-esteem is lost when they feel they have not lived up to their own expectations. For example, they may be disappointed in their inability to generate original or new ideas. The words of one teacher reveal such disappointment: "I became less creative and more tradition bound. Nothing was working anymore." Not only had she failed to live up to her own standards, she had also lost the support of a collegial faculty: "We [the faculty] became isolated, didn't chat about our teaching anymore. The faculty room was negative, full of gossip."

When loss of self-esteem is prolonged and intense, it can result in depression, a serious disorder that requires treatment. Burnout increases irritability. Minor frustrations can result in an explosion of anger. Victims of burnout are impatient, overly critical, suspicious, and convinced that everyone is out to make their lives difficult (Maslach, 1982).

Work Performance

> Some of the clock-punchers must have begun with admirable intentions; they must have enjoyed the camaraderie and occasionally even the kids. But they would not sacrifice their personal time to the cause: rather than quit ... they chose to cut corners, to scale back...to replace in essence, the scribbles and cross-outs of endeavor with the Liquid Paper of image. (Freedman, 1991, p. 227)

Burned-out teachers become increasingly less able to cope with the responsibilities and pressures of teaching. Although some teachers maintain that they care for their students, they are emotionally incapable of acting on those feelings (Abu-Hial & Salamen, as cited in Hewitt, 1993). During an interview, one teacher said, "I knew that I was failing the kids and I felt badly for them."

The quantity and quality of their work deteriorates. They no longer teach with enthusiasm or creativity; instead, they prepare stale, bookish presentations, giving the bare minimum or giving nothing at all (Maslach, 1982; Maslach & Leiter, 1997).

Students of burned-out teachers pay a high price. The lack of motivation and enthusiasm affects not only the burned-out teacher, but also the students for whom that teacher is responsible. Students are sentenced to teachers who display little enthusiasm for the subject they are teaching and who are seldom responsive to questions or needs. Teachers may deliver uninteresting and unimaginative lessons.

Not only do students receive inferior teaching, but often they are treated in a dehumanizing manner. Their teachers are often irritable, impatient, and quick to anger over minor frustrations. Teachers are inflexible in their responses, highly critical, and quick to judge students. They sit behind their desks, unapproachable and avoiding contact with students (Maslach, 1982; Stern & Cox, 1993). One teacher said, "I knew that I should be working with my students and felt guilty for not doing so. But I just couldn't give anymore."

Teachers experiencing burnout no longer spend extra time working with individuals. Little will be done to encourage student learning. A burned-out teacher, who has given up on a student, commented:

He's not motivated, doesn't do his work, so there's nothing I can do about it. If his parents don't care, why should I? I'm not wasting my time. He can just fail.

Students are perceptive. They can tell when a teacher does not care about them and does not want to teach. Students interviewed by Stern and Cox (1993) reported that teachers who demonstrated characteristics of burnout damaged the students' educational careers, particularly in the area of motivation. These students became more apathetic toward learning.

An interview with a high school teacher revealed the destructive "mirroring" effects that teacher burnout can have on students' attitudes and behavior.

The teachers' negative attitude trickles down to the way they treat the students. And the kids are a mirror image of the [teachers'] negative attitude. I've actually heard them [teachers] verbally abuse students. Tell them they're not worth anything, they should drop out of school—so it's a mirroring effect, like throwing a rock in a pond.... The kids are behavior problems, but the way they are treated fans the flames.

Burned-out teachers avoid work. According to one teacher, "Many of the teachers in my school are burned out. If it takes an extra effort to do anything, find out an answer to something, they will not do that." A response such as "If it's not in my contract, it's not my responsibility" is common. One teacher said, "We have a lot of absences and tardiness in our school, kids just get up and leave class, but teachers are so burned out that they don't bother to report them."

Students who are not motivated learners or who struggle to learn will not be provided with necessary encouragement or assistance. Those who are enthusiastic learners may experience boredom from not being challenged by the teachers. Students with behavioral or personal issues will not fare well with an uncaring, impatient, and inflexible teacher. All of the students, regardless of their motivation and abilities, will be hindered educationally in the classroom of a burned-out teacher.

A study by Dworkin (1987) reported that bright, high-achieving students are likely to suffer most from a burned-out teacher. Gifted children need a teacher who can stimulate them to heighten their achievements. Because teachers suffering from burnout are not willing to go beyond the requirements of minimal lessons, they do not provide the stimulation or enrichment needed to challenge high-achieving students. They may even feel threatened by a group of very bright students who may demand more interaction and stimulation from their teachers.

Some teachers spend more time with their fellow complainers than they do interacting with students. They contaminate faculty lounges with their criticisms of students, colleagues, parents, and principals. No person is spared their sharp-tongued, caustic remarks. Nothing more effectively destroys faculty morale than these individuals. A student teacher described the verbal destruction in her school's faculty room:

> The faculty room is awful. I expected to become part of professional conversations and learn a lot. Instead I am so disappointed. The teachers criticize the principal, make fun of parents, and are sarcastic about students. I have lost my heroes.

Personal Relationships

Teachers experiencing burnout may take their problems home and inflict their troubles and unhappiness on families and friends. When family and friends become weary of listening, the burned-out teacher accuses them of not being sympathetic. Eventually, the continuous negativity and lack of interest in others affects the teacher's relationships with family and colleagues. Family members and friends feel angry, neglected, and hurt. Family arguments, disagreements with friends, and marital conflict increase. Sometimes the result is divorce, lost friendships, and trouble with children (Maslach, 1982). As relationships deteriorate, teachers receive less support in their personal lives, thus compounding their problems. One teacher remarked:

> A lot of people I counted on for support weren't there for me. I think a lot about those lost friendships…but I isolated myself…can't blame other people.

Another teacher expressed profound grief over a lost friendship:

> It will make me cry to tell you. My very best friend, who always said I will be there when you need me, was not. Our close friendship disappeared. The impression I got was that she didn't want to be around someone who was miserable all the time. I didn't need solutions, just somebody to listen. That relationship was a close one, and I still grieve over it and how that happened.

At the other extreme are the burned-out teachers who do not talk about their problems at all. Instead, they withdraw to protect themselves from reliving the day's events and emotions. Family members feel shut out and confused. One teacher described her pattern of withdrawal:

> Now that I'm better I can see that I didn't help myself by not talking to anyone, especially my husband. He complained that I worked all the time. When I came home from work, I was exhausted and sat like a zombie in front of the TV. I didn't eat or sleep well. I lost a lot of weight and became ill. Finally, I left the school.

By withdrawing into silence, the teacher inadvertently created additional problems by setting up barriers to individuals who could have provided support.

Burnout has the potential to destroy marriages. One teacher tried to change jobs to solve a burnout problem. She described the conflict with her spouse:

> I found another job, but my [spouse] objected to my working out of town and having an apartment there. My [spouse] was not helpful, the way I would have been if the situation were reversed. It was my decision, I could have left. I started to think of what it would take to establish an apartment. It felt too much like a divorce. I looked for other options and found one.

In this case, the teacher found another opportunity, and she and her spouse grew closer because of the experience. Others are not so fortunate.

Spiritual

The final stage of burnout is spiritual despair. One teacher said she felt like she was "dropping into a black hole." A teacher teetering on the brink of burnout said, "I have to get out of this school before I topple over the edge." These teachers are describing the loss of balance or harmony in their lives.

The workplace occupies the majority of our waking hours, and for many individuals, it is the source of meaning and purpose in life. When workers are expected to "check their personal selves at the doors," they are prevented from bringing their most creative gifts to the job. The result is fear, anxiety, isolation, and apathy—the ingredients of spiritual poverty (Shipka, 1993).

Until recently, it was unusual to include the concept of spirituality in organizational life. Such concerns were considered separate from the rest of our lives (Barrentine, 1993). Yet the integration of work and personal life is essential to balance and harmony in our lives. Spiritual harmony occurs when personal needs, work responsibilities, and family obligations are balanced. Teachers who reported working in "burnout-free" schools cited the presence of opportunities for spiritual growth and development as key aspects of these schools (Brock, 1999).

COST TO THE ORGANIZATION

School administrators often fail to recognize the full impact of teacher burnout. Often the problem is ignored until it becomes so severe that parents and students complain and the administrator is forced to take action.

A few burned-out teachers change schools or quit teaching, giving up careers that were once a source of joy and personal identity. Principals are usually pleased when the teachers quit, feeling that they have been spared the trouble of the termination process and possible lawsuits (Maslach & Leiter, 1997).

Some teachers who experience burnout do not leave the schools. Instead, they remain on the job, feeling miserable and doing a disservice to their students and to the profession. They make minimal contributions to learning but heavy contributions to poor faculty morale. A few burned-out teachers can damage the climate and reduce the overall effectiveness of the school. Two teachers used a "poison" metaphor to describe the effect: "it's like dropping poison into a pool" and "[they're] the poison in Camelot."

Absenteeism is an additional problem. Teachers experiencing burnout tend to be absent in proportion to their level of distress. When teachers are absent, the financial burden on the school increases, and, more important, the education of students is interrupted.

The financial costs to the schools are in terms of high teacher turnover, absenteeism, and use of medical benefits. The intangible cost is the greatest loss, the long-term effect that poor teaching has on students. This is a problem that cannot be ignored.

Seeking Assistance

Teachers seldom seek assistance for burnout. First of all, burnout does not occur as a single event. It occurs slowly, over a period of time. Initially, teachers may be unaware of their burnout. Gradually, suspicion and paranoia may cloud their ability to make sound judgments and clear decisions. Teachers have difficulty identifying the situational cause of the problem. Instead, they believe that they or some other person is to blame, rather than the situation. For instance, they may feel that the kids are not motivated or that their parents do not care. One teacher described why she was leaving teaching: "I cared more about the kids than their parents did. How could I do a good job when the parents didn't show up, didn't participate. I got tired of taking care of other peoples' kids."

Teachers experiencing burnout may believe that only they have problems. Because they avoid interacting with colleagues, they do not realize that others may have the same difficulties. They believe that they are inadequate in some way and attempt to hide their distress. Findings in a study by Brock (1999) revealed that none of the teachers who had recovered from burnout had discussed their burnout problem with their principals. They handled the problem themselves, discussing it with family or colleagues. One teacher reported, "I toughed it out myself."

Finally, teachers are in a helping profession. They are expected to have answers to problems and to help others. Admitting that they need help may be a sign of incompetence or failure. They fear the loss of others' trust and respect (Maslach, 1982).

Stress Management Is Not the Solution

Teacher burnout is viewed by some individuals as an epidemic with serious consequences. Others think of teacher burnout as a convenient term for lazy teachers (Farber, 1991). Some principals may share their views. They view teacher burnout as an individual problem, failing to understand the organization's contribution to burnout. They equate burnout with disgruntled, lazy teachers who like to complain or with teachers who cannot handle the stress of teaching.

In the past, assuming that the problem was "owned" exclusively by the teachers, schools provided stress management workshops to assist teachers in solving their problem. The target was personal change. These workshops were usually ineffective, because the multiple sources of the problem were not identified. Although occasionally teachers can change their coping behaviors, they cannot individually effect changes in the organization. The actual causes of burnout are larger than they can handle. Burnout is a complex, multifaceted organizational issue, and it needs to be addressed as one.

Burnout can be minimized, even solved, by directing the focus of attention primarily to the organization and the work of teaching and secondarily to the individual teacher. As Albert Einstein said, "The significant problems we face cannot be solved at the same level of thinking we were at when we created them."

SUMMARY

The costs of teacher burnout are great. Teachers suffer loss of physical and emotional health. Relationships with family, friends, and colleagues suffer. Teachers feel out of balance spiritually, sinking into despair.

Burnout results in an inferior education for students. School administrators struggle with poor faculty morale, disgruntled parents, high absenteeism, and teacher turnover. The teaching profession loses gifted teachers.

Part II

RECOVERY AND PREVENTION

Igniting the Flames

Revitalization Strategies

A great flame follows a little spark.

—Dante

REVIVING THE BURNED-OUT TEACHER

A race car accelerates when the flow of fuel to the engine increases and a spark generates internal combustion. When the fuel tank is empty or the spark is diminished, the car slows and stops. In similar fashion, teachers without adequate fuel or the spark to ignite their enthusiasm cease to function. They quit working, either on or off the job.

Teachers struggling with burnout have the potential for recovery. The task of the principal, faced with burned-out teachers, is to discover a source of fuel and a spark that will reenergize them.

Confronting the Issue

Burnout is no longer simply "a personal problem." Today we realize that burnout is a workplace problem that requires both individual and organizational efforts to resolve it.

The first step in eradicating burnout is acknowledging that burnout exists in schools and that it is a correctable and preventable problem. In the words of a teacher:

My principal should have acknowledged that the teachers in the school were miserable and done something to address the issue. People were calling in sick, being absent a lot. The signs were there. In his first year, teachers spoke up at the faculty meeting. As the year progressed, the principal talked, while teachers sat, arms folded, and said nothing. He had a responsibility to problem-solve. He should have been in halls, in classrooms...acknowledged our misery and helped us. Instead, he retreated too. He went into his office and closed the door.

Causes of burnout may be beyond the control of the building administrator. Issues that exist at the district level or those resulting from national perception are beyond the province of a principal. However, many of the causes of burnout are within the principal's direct control, and steps can be taken to assist teachers in a recovery process. An outline of the recovery process includes:

+ Recognizing burnout as a school problem
+ Identifying burnout symptoms
+ Assessing the causes of burnout
+ Taking steps to eradicate causes
+ Evaluating effectiveness

Awareness of the Symptoms

As "fog creeps in on little cat feet," so burnout creeps into schools, hiding in corners and catching participants unaware. An experienced and dedicated teacher described a burnout experience:

I have been mentally changed by the burnout experience. I used to see the world through rose-colored glasses, imma- ture, I guess. I know now that just doing the right thing won't get you a reward. Presented with burnout symptoms again, I will act more quickly. I learned a lot from this experience.

Burnout has the potential to spread, sweeping through a school and destroying faculty morale in its path. Principals who maintain close contact and interact regularly with their teachers will be in a position to recognize early symptoms, such as changes in behavior, attitude, and attendance. Curtailing the symptoms in their early stages may prevent a widespread and serious problem.

Determine the Causes

A key to recognizing burnout is the behavior of the faculty. Observations in classrooms and hallways as well as listening to and talking with teachers and students can provide valuable clues. One teacher described a principal who did just the opposite:

> My principal could have acknowledged that he had a staff of people who were miserable…and done something to fix that…I thought he had a responsibility to people who worked there. There were people sick all the time. I would like to have had him do some problem solving about it. I could spend a month and never even see the man.

One teacher who struggled with burnout for several years said, "I wanted to be rescued by somebody." She described actions that she would have liked her principal to take:

> I would like to have had him in the halls…in my classroom, and not just put some note in my box, "Good job." I'd like to have had him say something specific about what I was doing, acknowledge the fact that I and everybody else was in a miserable situation and give some credit for it. I was disappointed in him. He needed to be in the classrooms, helping us because we were alone. Everybody was alone. He should have said, I have to get this faculty working together. If I had somebody [like me] begging for two years [to make changes]…I'd figure out a way to deal with that person.

When burnout occurs, teachers feel that they no longer have control over their situations. They want their principal to understand their problems and to provide assistance. Teachers who have experienced burnout or witnessed it in colleagues are often able to identify the source of the problem and to suggest solutions to remedy it.

A variety of data collection strategies are available, such as:

◆ Dispelling the myths

◆ Systematic observations of faculty

◆ Open-ended discussions with small groups of teachers

◆ Feedback from students and parents

◆ Exit interviews with teachers

◆ Burnout inventories

Dispelling the Myths

Burnout is usually treated as a school secret. Everyone knows that some teachers are suffering burnout, but nobody is willing to discuss it. Teachers are reluctant to admit that they are suffering burnout symptoms for fear of being misjudged or losing face. Consequently, the first task of the principal is to dispel the myths.

Observations

The purpose of observations is to document stress-related behaviors and symptoms. The focus of the observation is (a) the symptoms exhibited and (b) the context in which they occurred. Consider the following example: During three half-hour observations of a seventh-grade art class, the teacher used sarcasm with students and displayed anger by shouting. The 25 students in the class had inadequate materials, argued about sharing, and yelled out questions while the teacher gave directions. The observations reveal stress-related behaviors (i.e., sarcasm, anger, and shouting) as well as school conditions that may be producing them (i.e., inadequate resources, large class size, and discipline problems).

DISCUSSING BURNOUT WITH GROUPS AND INDIVIDUALS

Discussing burnout is a necessary and effective step in both recovery and prevention. In a study by Brock (1999), teachers, counselors, and principals rated "discussing burnout" as an effective strategy in "reviving" teachers and preventing future occurrences.

Focusing the discussion on school issues will remove the blame and stigma from the condition. Teachers should be encouraged to engage in the discussion.

Feedback From Students and Parents

When teachers are suffering burnout, student learning is affected. Continuous feedback indicating low student performance, chronic discipline problems, or complaints from students and their parents may signal teacher burnout. Although most teachers experience occasional problems with students or complaints from parents, repeated and serious incidents should be investigated.

Exit Interviews

An exit interview provides an opportunity for a principal to determine the reasons for a teacher's departure from a school. Constant turnover is an indicator of a serious case of burnout in a school.

Burnout Inventories

If tension and distrust exist in a school, a burnout inventory may be the best means of identifying problem areas. Teachers need to be confident that their responses to such an inventory will be anonymous and free from repercussions. Although a burnout inventory should be tailored to the individual needs of a school, sample items are suggested in Table 2 (see Resources).

Acknowledging Issues Beyond Your Control

Situations "beyond the control of the principal" may result from an accumulation of issues that spill over from a personal life or from district policies that the principal cannot change. In a study by Brock (1999), teachers were frustrated by the lack of special education teachers available to assist them with special education students mainstreamed into their classrooms. Other teachers cited inequitable salaries as contributing to their burnout. Clearly, these are examples of issues that are beyond the power of the building principal. Yet having the principal listen to the concerns, acknowledge their significance, and represent those concerns at the district level is critical. The teachers may not have their problems solved, but at least they know that their concerns are being heard and taken seriously.

When burnout stems solely from a personal issue, assistance may take the form of listening. For serious personal problems, it may be necessary to refer the teacher for professional assistance. One principal gave the following example:

> One of my most conscientious teachers suddenly started arriving late, missing deadlines and functions, and seemed distant and distraught. I invited her to meet with me and asked her what was going on in her life. She started to cry and told me that her husband's drinking was creating chaos in her home life. She couldn't handle the pressures at home combined with school anymore. I helped her find a social agency to assist her family.

People become burned out when they feel powerless, trapped by others' demands, and confronted with regulations and endless demands. Regaining autonomy and personal control is important to recovery. Some teachers try to overcome burnout alone. However, if the burnout is the result of an organizational issue, they will not be completely successful without the assistance of the principal.

Teachers Fueling Their Own Flames

Years ago canaries were used in the coal mines as a signal to the miners that the air had become toxic. When the canaries stopped singing, the miners knew it was time to get out (Barrentine, 1993). Some teachers realize when their own canary has stopped singing and know that they need to act on their own behalf.

If an organization will not or cannot address burnout issues, teachers may attempt to improve situations that they can control. In one school, the teachers reported that they overcame burnout by taking "charge of their lives and their teaching."

Individuals may cope with and overcome burnout by exerting active control over their situation rather than passively acquiescing. They reorder their private lives, engage in self-reflection, address personal problems, and develop a more positive attitude. They change their work routine and redefine their goals.

STRATEGIES TO REVITALIZE

Most of the causes of burnout require changes within the organization and assistance from the principal. Strategies that principals can use to revitalize teachers include:

+ Change the teacher's environment
+ Create support networks
+ Provide direct administrative assistance
+ Decrease workload
+ Change administrative behavior
+ Change school policies and procedures
+ Encourage professional growth
+ Increase school safety
+ Provide time away from school
+ Initiate a transfer to a new school
+ Provide a transfer within teaching field
+ Suggest leaving the teaching profession

Change the Teachers' Environment

Changes in physical environment and teaching assignments work wonders in revitalizing teachers who are slipping toward burnout. Even minor actions can enhance confidence and self-esteem.

New Surroundings. For most individuals, changing surroundings decreases boredom and stimulates a fresh outlook. A different view from the window, new next-door neighbors, and a change in room arrangement can be invigorating. Cleaning out accumulated clutter, throwing away outdated materials, and reorganizing belongings restores a sense of order and control. One principal said:

> Most of the teachers in my school were long-time veterans in the building. I think some of them arrived when the building was built...their rooms and their attitudes reflected it. You can imagine the resistance I received when I announced several classroom changes. But once they moved and settled into their new locations, many of them told me that they felt recharged and refreshed by cleaner rooms and new surroundings.

Change of Grade Levels or Subject Areas. Changing grade levels or subject areas revitalizes teachers. Teachers who periodically change stay more engaged and interested in their work. Prerequisites include being informed of the impending change and adequate preparation to do the job (Brock, 1999; Reinhold, 1996). One principal reported:

> I was at my wits' end with my second-grade teacher. She was negative, irritable, impatient...classes were non-descript. Anyway, one day she came in and asked if she could change grade levels...that she was tired of teaching primary students and wanted to teach older students. I took a chance and moved her to sixth grade...wow, what a difference. She became one of my best teachers.

Teaching Relationships. Reassigning classes to enable teachers to collaborate in team teaching or other forms of shared teaching provides a welcome challenge for some individuals. Sharing perspectives with another teacher is energizing.

Change in Instruction. Some teachers benefit from instructional changes, such as a new curriculum, different textbooks, and innovative instructional methods. One teacher said "[she] revitalized [her]self by revising [her] courses and selecting all new material."

Support Networks

Support Groups. Teachers who are struggling with burnout need to talk about it in a safe setting with others who understand their problems. Emotional support through discussions among colleagues and support networks plays a significant part in the recovery from burnout (Kijai & Totten, 1995; Reinhold, 1996).

Senior Faculty. Beginning teachers in particular are prone to discouragement that may eventually trigger burnout. Senior faculty are important sources of encouragement and support for beginning teachers and newcomers.

School Counselors. School counselors can provide support for teachers who are struggling with school as well as personal problems. Administrators, in a study by Brock and Ponec (1998), reported that their counselors sought out and offered assistance to staff members. Although not their primary responsibility, the additional benefit that the counselors provided was highly valued by the teachers and principals.

Direct Assistance With Discipline, Teaching, and Attitudes

Student and Parent Problems. Chronic problems with student discipline and oppositional parents are major causes of teacher burnout. These problems can be reduced by learning effective strategies to deal with student discipline and by learning how to work cooperatively with parents (Kijai & Totten, 1995; Townley et al., 1991).

Reviving Teaching. Stagnation is another frequent cause of burnout. As one teacher said, "Nothing I do seems to work anymore." Direct assistance in learning and trying out new teaching strategies can revitalize teachers. Another technique involves changing the teachers' focus from content and process of teaching to the students being taught. The intent is to create a radical shift in teaching philosophy and a subsequent change in teaching style. Changes such as these require effort and the acceptance of risk on the part of both the teachers and the principals. Coaching and modeling by the principal can be beneficial. In order for growth to occur, the relationship between principal and teachers needs to be one of trust and mutual respect. Teachers will not experiment unless they feel safe to make mistakes and to experience occasional failures.

Attitude. Some capable teachers create burnout by their own negative thinking. They focus on what is wrong rather than what is right, failure rather than success. They become discouraged. Even though their abilities are obvious to others, they fail to recognize their strengths, talents, and successes unless they are pointed out. Such assistance as positive reinforcement and teaching teachers to identify their own successes can be powerful tools. One principal suggested, "Work with teachers in their strength areas; focus on what they do well and help them do that better."

Decreased Workload

Learning to Say No. Some teachers create their own excessive workload. They like to be involved, have many ideas, and cannot say "no" to any new project. Reinhold (1996) compared such teachers to the characters in the *I Love Lucy* episode in which Lucy and Ethel were boxing candies in a factory and could not keep up with the conveyer belt. Teachers who overextend themselves by trying to do everything cannot keep up with the endless conveyer belt of demands. Even though they are frustrated, their need to please, to be liked, or to be involved motivates them to continue to overextend themselves. Beginning teachers and teachers new to a school often fall victim to this syndrome in their efforts to be accepted. One principal cautioned:

> Educate beginning teachers about the perils of burnout and learning to say no discriminately. Also, protect beginning teachers by weighting different committee assignments. Don't give the most demanding jobs to new teachers...not fair, but often seasoned staff will want to give [the tough jobs] to the new kid.

Permission to Relax. Experienced teachers who tend to overextend will benefit from discussions of burnout and how to provide balance in their work and home life. Teachers may need to be told that it is OK and important to take time off to relax (Maslach, 1982). One principal reported an example of a teacher who came to work every day before 7 a.m. and stayed until 5 or 6 p.m. Eventually, she became resentful of colleagues who did not share her lengthy workday, as though they were shirking their duty.

The Workaholic School Culture. Some schools actually foster a culture of teacher overload. Teachers learn that the cultural expectation is for faculty to arrive early, stay late, and take a lot home. One first-year teacher reported, "I am viewed with raised eyebrows and a quick exchange of glances when I leave right away after school to pick up my child from daycare. My principal tells me to go, but my colleagues make me feel guilty—like I'm not carrying my load."

Overloaded by the Principal. Sometimes the principal unwittingly creates the imbalance or overload. Many teachers suffer because of classloads, committee assignments, and duties required as part of their job. Principals need to be aware of the workload of each teacher and to make every attempt to equalize work. Given the lack of personnel in some schools, this may require creativity on the part of the principal.

Administrative Behavior

Hostile Environment. The workplace is where teachers spend many waking hours. It is part of their identity, where they find a purpose to their lives. When work conditions are sterile and teachers are expected to check their personal selves at the door, they are prevented from bringing their most creative selves to work. Such a work setting spawns a spiritual poverty, denoted by fear, anxiety, isolation, and apathy (Shipka, 1993).

Administrators can create hostile environments through their treatment of teachers. Lapses in two-way communication spawn negative environments. Failure to provide personal attention, recognition for work, fairness, or support is cited as a factor in teacher burnout. Teachers fear repercussions for calling in sick, needing a day off to care for a sick child, or handling personal matters. Principals may be unaware that their actions are problematic. Remedies are open discussions, exit interviews, and inventories to determine burnout causes. Once specific administrative behaviors or procedures are identified as burnout factors, the principal can initiate changes to create a more favorable work environment.

A Positive Response. A positive attitude is contagious. Principals who are visible in the building, greet people, converse with teachers, and are enthusiastic and smiling send a positive message to teachers. As several teachers pointed out, the principal is responsible for creating a positive work environment:

- ◆ The principal should be visible in the building
- ◆ The principal should not complain
- ◆ The principal should focus on building strengths
- ◆ The principal should plan times for faculty to play and social-ize together
- ◆ The principal should call teachers by name, care about them, and know what is important to them
- ◆ The principal should be willing to listen and be open to others

Professional Growth

Teachers may become burned out from staying in one place too long. Making changes in teaching assignments, obtaining further education, and networking have the potential to rejuvenate interest and revitalize work. Taking a class or workshop, attending a confer-ence, or networking with others in the same grade level or subject area may stimulate new interest.

Assigning a student teacher to a teacher whose interest appears to be waning could provide a professional challenge. Teaching a stu-dent teacher is fulfilling, a chance to share accumulated knowledge and experiences as well as to refine skills by reevaluating perfor-mance. An eager, questioning student teacher brings a fresh per-spective and prompts renewed interest (Reinhold, 1996).

Increased Personal Safety

Working in violent school environments is destructive to the emotional well-being of teachers. If a teacher has suffered a violent physical attack, the need for immediate medical as well as emotional assistance is critical. Teachers who suffer burnout because of violent work situations need to be transferred to less stressful, nonviolent schools. A new setting will provide an opportunity to renew moti-vation and refresh the psyche. In addition, opportunities to discuss experiences with others may assist individuals in sorting out and working through the violence they have encountered.

Escape From School

Constant contact with large numbers of people is an intense experience that cannot be endured for long periods of time without some mental escape. Time to relax is essential if teachers are to maintain enthusiasm about teaching. Outside weekend and evening activities are important. Holidays, vacations, and summer breaks have a revitalizing effect. Some teachers find that travel is stimulating. Sabbatical leaves provide opportunities to become refreshed as well as to engage in additional training or other professional growth (Gaziel, 1995).

Change of Schools

Burnout is often the result of a mismatch between the teacher and the school. Sometimes teachers do not fit into a school's culture or agree with all the aspects of the school's administration.

A move may enable a teacher to select a more compatible teaching environment. A new location may help reestablish a career with more balance and greater enthusiasm. As testimony to the value of change, one teacher said:

My former principal and I didn't agree on anything. I was miserable all the time. My new principal recognizes my leadership ability and has given me responsibilities for initiating new programs. I'm happy now.

Another teacher reported a similar experience: "I left a negative school with little administrative support and…[moved to a school with] a principal who was sensitive to my workload."

Change Within the Profession

Sometimes individuals who become burned out in K-12 schools move to other roles in the profession and discover more appropriate settings for their gifts. They find roles in administration, counseling, or a central office to be more satisfying. Still others move on to community colleges, four-year colleges, and universities (Huberman, 1993).

Leaving the Teaching Profession

The most drastic response to burnout is leaving the teaching profession altogether. For most teachers, leaving the field is not easy.

For some, the choice follows the realization that they are not suited to the profession. For others, leaving is an admission of failure. The tragedy lies in the fact that the failure may not be that of the teacher.

Principals, weary of struggling with low-performing teachers, are often anxious to see them leave. However, a danger lies in hasty judgments. If burnout symptoms are mistaken for incompetence, the profession is destined to lose gifted teachers.

SUMMARY

Burnout is not a new phenomenon. Researchers have been studying and writing about it for more than 20 years. Yet in many schools, its existence continues to be attributed to teacher flaws rather than to organizational causes. Rather than mourning the loss of dedicated teachers, some principals rejoice when they leave. Other principals choose to confront burnout, to resolve the causes at their source, and to revive talented but suffering teachers.

Burnout is often a symptom of workplace issues that principals can identify and correct. Given the destructive effects of burnout on both students and teachers, the time and effort spent in facilitating recovery are clearly warranted.

Guardian of the Flame

The Principal's Role

We must be the change we wish to see in the world.

—Ghandi

THE PRINCIPAL'S INFLUENCE

The role of the principal is to create a school environment conducive to learning and satisfying to teachers and students. Although extensive literature exists on students' learning conditions, little interest has been paid to teachers' working conditions and their effect on teacher performance.

Principals have control over organizational factors that include: (a) administrative actions, (b) the school's climate, and (c) teachers' working conditions. By leading, directing, and inspiring change and coordination, principals have the power to create a healthy and exciting learning environment—one that reduces the likelihood of burnout. To create satisfying working conditions, principals need to examine the operation of the school and the degree to which it meets the expectations and needs of teachers. Satisfying working conditions are displayed in Table 3 (see Resources).

According to Herzberg's Motivation-Hygiene Theory, one set of factors (motivators) produces satisfaction, whereas another set (hygienes) produces dissatisfaction. Positive events were dominated by references to achievement, recognition (verbal), the work itself (challenging), responsibility, and advancement (promotion) (Herzberg, Mausner, & Snyderman, 1959). Negative events were dominated by references to interpersonal relations with superiors and peers, technical supervision, company policy and administration, working conditions, and personal life (Hoy & Miskel, 1991). Teachers who leave teaching because of burnout report dissatisfaction with all of the hygiene factors (company policy and administration, supervision, salary, interpersonal relations) and with the motivational factors of recognition, advancement, and achievement (Frataccia & Hennington, 1982). For a wholesome working environment, the school's operation must respond to hygiene and motivational needs.

Principals can exert influence by assisting teachers in satisfying both hygiene and motivational needs. Principals can ensure that teachers' hygiene needs are met through school policies, consistent procedures, and ongoing supervision. Motivational needs are met by placing teachers in appropriate teaching settings, offering professional growth opportunities, and providing time and resources to achieve success.

Morale as Predictor

The greatest predictor of student success is teacher attitude. Although curriculum, pedagogy, and teacher talent are important, teacher morale is the key. Learning does not occur in a school filled with unhappy, burned-out teachers.

Most teachers do not become burned out, leave schools, or quit teaching because they dislike the students or hate teaching. They leave because they cannot work with the principal, the school is poorly administered, or they are treated unfairly. One teacher explained why she planned to leave her school:

> This is my first year in this school and hopefully my last. The majority of the staff is extremely burned out and would have a hard time mustering up to becoming good teachers. I'm not burned out yet, but I can't make a difference with this administration.

Successful principals create an environment in which teachers want to teach. They view teachers as the most important link to student learning and create an environment in which people are valued and are doing the work for which they are best suited. They focus on people, recognize and develop teachers' talents, develop strong relationships, and lead by inspiring. One teacher explained that "teachers [in this school] were hired with ability and desire and that isn't gone. It just needs to be brought out by the administration." Figure 2 (see Resources) represents a continuum of organizational health.

Successful Principals

How do principals develop and sustain positive teacher morale? One teacher offered the following advice:

> Smile. Call us by name. Act like you care and know what is important to us. Bring small groups of teachers together to work on tasks. Provide positive feedback. Use conflict resolution to resolve issues. Survey the faculty regularly to find out what people have to say and how things are improving.
>
> Be in classrooms and point out good things that are happening—specific things. Don't patronize. Be available. If you see someone in distress, unhappy, and retreating from others, reach out and help them.

Following are specific administrative strategies recommended by teachers as deterrents to burnout.

Provide Time to Teach. A teacher's job is to teach. Yet lack of time to teach is a major stress factor for teachers. Here is a typical teacher complaint:

> I don't have enough time to teach with all the interruptions. I seldom have my entire class in the room at the same time.... We have constant interruptions with announcements and kids coming and going.

To be effective, teachers need uninterrupted time to teach. Teachers applaud and acknowledge the importance of services for students. Their concern is with poorly designed schedules that produce discontinuity for students and impair their learning. Simple changes, such as limiting intercom use, will be welcomed by teachers. Schedules should provide adequate time and appropriate sequencing for teaching and delivery of auxiliary services.

Minimize Duties. Feeling overwhelmed by the workload is a major factor in teacher burnout. Teachers feel as though their job is never finished. There are always more papers to correct and lesson plans to be made. They are deluged with paperwork from the office. Minimizing paperwork and administrative tasks frees teachers to spend more time working with students and teaching.

Some teachers feel more like babysitters (or security guards) than professionals. They spend much of their time supervising students before and after school, during passing periods, at lunch, and on the playground. Clearly, supervision is necessary, and student safety must never be compromised. However, teacher morale can be improved by relieving teachers of supervisory duties that take time away from planning and preparing for classes.

A careful examination of current supervisory duties may reveal aspects that can be eliminated, reduced, or reassigned to nonteaching personnel. Solutions may include: (a) reducing the need for supervision by changes in scheduling to reduce the numbers of students congregating before and after school, during passing periods, and in the cafeteria and (b) the use of paraprofessionals and security personnel in supervision (Potter, 1995).

Maximize Encouragement. Teachers seldom know the impact they have on students. No measure of quality exists at the end of a hard day. Their only reinforcement comes from self-assessment, an occasional glimpse of success in a student's response, and infrequent praise from parents. Although some fortunate teachers have opportunities for collaboration with peers, in many schools, principals are the only reliable referent available for teachers in judging their work. Consequently, principals need to provide reinforcement and encouragement for teachers (Blase & Kirby, 1992).

Teachers value personal, job-related compliments from their principals. Praise is a powerful strategy in influencing teachers' work and level of satisfaction. It enhances teacher morale, attitudes toward students, instructional practices, and the amount of effort put forth. Praise, however, needs to be personalized, specific, related to a professional role, and sincere.

A second powerful strategy is personal attention from the principal. Teachers want their principals to spend time talking with them, sharing their goals for the school and listening to their concerns and ideas. Personal attention makes teachers feel that their contributions are important and that they are important members of the team (Blase & Kirby, 1992).

Principals who encourage teachers to try new things are using another influential strategy. If an idea fails, they promptly respond with positive reinforcement through increased attention, notes of encouragement, and verbal assurances to try again (Winter & Sweeney, 1994).

Although powerful, these simple forms of reinforcement are underused by principals. By not finding time to offer simple praise, to pay attention, and to encourage new ideas, principals miss opportunities to reinforce and encourage quality performance that builds teachers' confidence and satisfaction (Blase & Kirby, 1992; Brock & Grady, 1997; Winter & Sweeney, 1994).

Show Concern for Individuals. Principals demonstrate that they care through their use of body language, informal conversation, moral support, constructive criticism, and assistance. Principals who care smile, show enthusiasm, limit teaching interruptions, greet everyone, are available for assistance, and make one feel welcome in the office. They do not address the entire staff about negative concerns when the entire staff is not responsible for those concerns (Winter & Sweeney, 1994).

Provide Recognition. All workers, including teachers, want recognition for their work. They want their supervisors to notice what they are doing and that they are doing it well. Teachers want their principals to acknowledge their accomplishments (Winter & Sweeney, 1994).

Teachers tend toward burnout when they feel that their work is devoid of recognition. These feelings are fostered by principals' actions or inactions, parent criticism, and societal blame for inadequacies in the public schools.

Principals can override these feelings by (a) recognizing work done well; (b) acknowledging teachers' competencies by providing leadership responsibilities; (c) establishing a cooperative atmosphere where teachers help, support, and congratulate each other for their successes; and (d) not interfering in task completion (Friesen et al., 1988).

Treat Teachers Fairly. Teachers feel that enforcement of policies and rules is essential. Rules should be followed by everyone, regardless of status. When teachers perceive favoritism, particularly toward influential parents or community members, it diminishes the trust in the fairness of the principal (Winter & Sweeney, 1994).

Fairness is also reflected in division of teacher workloads. One teacher said, "I moved to a school with an administrator who was more sensitive to my workload." Since workload is a clear factor in stress and feelings of loss of control, principals need a clear picture of each teacher's workload and the ability of each teacher to handle the load. These factors need to be considered before assigning additional duties (Starnaman & Miller, 1992).

Show Enthusiasm. According to one teacher, "The principal shouldn't complain." Teachers need a principal who is a cheerleader—demonstrating enthusiasm, cheerfulness, and optimism.

Communicate. Teachers want to know what is going on in the building. They want to have an opportunity to provide input. Daily bulletins, containing contributions from everyone on the school staff, keep everyone up to date. One teacher said, "When I suggested a daily bulletin [to the principal] at the beginning of the year, he asked me why...he didn't think we'd have enough information to put into the bulletin." Faculty bulletins and memos from the principal are quick and efficient means of providing information.

Teachers in buildings with low morale frequently comment on the lack of communication provided through faculty meetings. One teacher said,

> Staff meetings are not held [at our school] because of the antagonism of the teachers toward the administration—once in a while an assistant administrator holds one, but not very often.

Faculty meetings, organized within a time frame and guided by an agenda, provide opportunities for discussion of important issues. One teacher commented on the importance of communication:

If I were principal, I would have a representative from each department and meet with them on a weekly basis...to keep communication lines open and include [teachers] in major decisions. Half the time [teachers] don't know what's going on.

Strategies for increasing teacher input include:

1. Small advisory committees that meet monthly to discuss problems and suggest solutions

2. Twenty-five-minute stand-up staff meetings before school during which everyone meets for a quick update

3. Lunch or dinner workshops to share ideas

4. A quick, anonymous survey of what is and is not working

5. Weekly staff meetings that focus on a specific theme (McGuire, 1993)

Engage Teachers. Teachers want to provide input into decisions that affect them. They appreciate participating in important decisions about their teaching and working conditions.

However, distinctions should be made between issues that require teacher input and other issues that merely consume time. Some principals, in their zeal to involve teachers in shared decision making, have merely added another duty to teachers' responsibilities—committee work. Teachers find themselves overburdened with incessant committee meetings (Potter, 1995).

Grant Autonomy. Good leaders share their vision, determine key goals, chart a course of action, provide resources, and then allow teachers to chart their own paths to goal accomplishment. They discover teachers' natural talents and then utilize those talents to the advantage of the organization and teachers.

A student studying to become a principal suggested a coaching model:

Stimulate enthusiasm, decide who plays each position, then get off the field and let the players carry the ball. Plan "timeouts" to evaluate the situation, revise strategies, and reinforce actions.

Teachers who are treated as knowledgeable professionals, whose input is valued, and who are allowed to exert judgment in how work is accomplished are more satisfied with their work.

Be Supportive. Research demonstrates that burnout is decreased when teachers feel supported by their principals. One teacher's comments follow:

> The teachers have a negative attitude because they're not receiving strong administrative support...it trickles down to the way they treat the students. The problem would become better in a short period of time if the teachers felt that they were supported by the administration.

Principals' support is related to decreased role ambiguity and role conflict. Supportive principals are interested in teachers' work, show active support, and are receptive to teachers' ideas. They allow teachers to become influential in the decision-making process. Principals who attempt to be supportive by sharing "war stories" and commiserating may actually increase student depersonalization, a negative response to students (Starnaman & Miller, 1992).

Teachers expect support from their principals when they experience problems with parents or community members. Knowing that they can rely on solid, unwavering support from their principal creates a sense of trust. The slightest sense of hesitancy or lack of support on the part of the principal destroys that trust (Winter & Sweeney, 1994).

One teacher spoke of teachers no longer disciplining students because their actions are not supported:

> If a teacher sends an individual to the office the student is considered innocent and the teacher is put on the spot and has to justify [actions] in front of the student and possibly parents...the teachers, are [no longer] addressing issues.
>
> One teacher reported a gun...security backed up the administration...said it [didn't exist] or was plastic, maybe the kid was just reaching for car keys.

Well-meaning principals may inadvertently lose trust when they are trying to help. A teacher who was experiencing problems with a parent explained:

My principal was shocked when I told him that I was uncomfortable with the meetings he had with the parent. He said he was just trying to help by listening to the parent's concerns...but I wasn't there and it felt like he was agreeing and sympathizing with them.

The story might have ended differently if the principal had assumed the role of facilitator and invited both parties to a meeting to resolve the conflict.

Ensure Safety. Physical safety is a prerequisite to effective teaching. Teachers cannot teach when they fear for their safety and the safety of their students. The soundness of the school's administration can be measured by the amount of teacher victimization that occurs (Gottfredson & Gottfredson, 1985). One teacher offered suggestions to improve faculty morale regarding personal safety:

[If I were principal] I would add more security...and a zero-tolerance policy...even though it's hard to maintain. I'd find more money to give [teachers] extra hazardous duty pay. They need more for putting up with [the situation].

Another suggested getting "serious" about the possibility of a crisis:

Our principal hasn't even [discussed] our crisis plan. We were supposed to go over it, but the principal put it on the back burner and said they know where it's at if they want to read it.

If safety is an issue, the first step is a risk assessment to determine necessary precautions.

Provide Staff Development. The words of a principal emphasize the importance of staff development in the prevention of burnout:

Schools in which teachers do not continue to learn are breeding grounds for being disgruntled. The key is keeping your staff learning and growing.

A contributing factor to teachers' lack of enthusiasm and burnout is the lack of continuous professional growth. Although most schools have required scheduled inservice activities, these activities do not constitute serious and sustained professional development. Although they may provide useful information, they fail to address individual needs, interest areas, or developmental career stages.

Instead, teachers need to develop their own plans based on interests and perceived deficits as well as the style of learning most suitable for them. Although the principal may act as facilitator, teachers prefer to choose professional development activities personally, rather than working out a plan with the principal or having a plan imposed by the principal (Richardson & Sistrunk, 1988).

Be Decisive. Decisive leaders have schools that are well organized, orderly, and safe. They know when to cease discussion and make a decision. They also recognize situations that require decisions made solely by the principal. Decisive leaders base their decisions on students' needs, have the strength of their convictions, and stand by their decisions in the face of controversy.

Decisive leaders understand the need for structure in the school. Policies, procedures, and rules create a structure so that order is maintained and learning can occur. A teacher, disappointed by the laissez-faire attitude of the principal, commented on the importance of order for kids living in chaos:

> We didn't have enough books, any books for the first month and a half, so the kids were working crossword puzzles... no rulers, calculators, or computer...we begged and borrowed to get materials for them. The district spent the whole summer planning this [program], but when it came down to it, they needed another year to get everything in place.

Keep the Building Clean. A clean, well-maintained building sends a strong message regarding the importance of education. Teachers who work in dirty, disheveled, and poorly maintained buildings soon feel that they and their work are not very important.

Know Thyself. The principal's education, experience, personality, and personal issues combine to influence leadership style and administrative behavior. In turn, the principal's administrative style and behavior affect teacher satisfaction and morale.

One teacher suggested improving morale by engaging teachers in school responsibilities: "[If I were principal] I'd distribute some of the responsibilities...have [teachers] in charge of some things and attach an accountability factor to that."

Principals who lack recent teaching experience or whose education appears less than current will have diminished credibility with teachers. One teacher provided the following example:

> Our administrator has been with the district for a number of years...but the last administrative course he took was well over 20 years ago [and]...he hasn't had any high school [teaching] experience for well over 20 years. [It's like] parenting a child if you've never been around children.... Morale is extremely low...and dropping because of lack of administrative support and knowledge....We went to the superintendent...but there is nothing they can do to remove him.

Personality is an additional factor in principals' expectations for others. Principals whose own lives consist of long working hours and little time for family, recreation, and relaxation may treat others in accordance with their own "workaholic" norms, failing to recognize the need for teachers to have balanced lives.

Occasionally, principals' work-related or personal problems affect their performance and, consequently, that of their staff. Suffering from burnout themselves, they are incapable of providing support for teachers. One teacher attributed the faculty's low morale to the principal's burnout:

> The principal himself is [suffering] major burnout. I think that's why he leaves the building all the time. Doesn't tell anybody where he is...there's no administrator on duty. He has told me a few times that he's sick, has a headache and needs to leave. He came into the situation with personal baggage, just went through a horrible divorce before he started his job.

A Burned-Out Faculty

Sometimes principals assume positions in schools where many of the teachers are suffering burnout. Before initiating changes to promote recovery, the new principal will need to determine the causes by investigating a number of factors, such as:

1. The prevailing school norms (culture and climate)
2. Current policies and procedures
3. Attitudes and expectations of parents, students, and community members
4. Historical issues
5. Information regarding the previous principals
6. Demands and constraints of district governing bodies and officials (Brock & Grady, 1995)

Discussions with teachers, both individually and in small groups, will reveal valuable information. However, teachers may initially be distrustful and reluctant to reveal information, depending upon their relationships with previous principals. One teacher suggested gathering information and then working with teachers during the summer:

> I would definitely be working with the teachers over the summer, find some money to pay them to come back [to work on] some of the problems...involve the teachers, identify the problems, do major problem solving on the issues, get a solution.

Individuals With Burnout

When the percentage of teachers who exhibit burnout symptoms is small, the focus moves to individual problems and solutions. Burnout causes and remedies are identifiable through systematic observations and conversations with individual teachers. In most cases, teachers who are truly burned out will welcome and respond to assistance. Those who need a career change will probably be unresponsive or resistant.

Serendipitous Benefits

Not all nonproductive or unsuccessful teachers suffer from burnout. Some teachers enter the profession, not because they have a burning desire to teach, but simply because they need a job. They may be in the wrong profession. However, efforts to revive teachers who are suffering from burnout may produce benefits for all teachers.

Not all teachers who eventually become highly successful enter the field with burning enthusiasm. After all, many new teachers are "twenty-something," poised on the threshold of adulthood. Often, enthusiasm for teaching develops as the young teacher matures and gains experience and confidence. Other teachers may have had difficult beginnings or inappropriate placements that sidetracked their development. Delivering personal attention and encouragement bears the promise of awakening dormant potential in the most unlikely individuals. One principal reported such a story:

> She was a teacher who blended into the wall. From the very beginning, she exhibited very little enthusiasm toward her teaching and even less toward the kids. When I counseled her about her behavior, she became more sullen. One day I noticed her talent in creative writing…and I encouraged her to teach a creative writing lesson to her students. The results were remarkable…for the first time I saw excitement. I moved her to a different grade level and a position that enabled her to use her writing talents. The change was unbelievable…her classes were exciting, her confidence grew…her students produced extraordinary results.

Another principal discovered a teacher in a wrong career during her campaign to eradicate burnout. In this case, the perseverance of the principal created a situation where everyone benefited.

> Janet had been teaching for twenty-some years but never very successfully. She kept up-to-date professionally and was obviously trying to do a good job. Yet, regardless of grade level, subject, additional training, and personal determination, she simply couldn't interact with the students.
>
> Observations and conversations revealed that Janet was always first to volunteer for faculty committees but refused to be spokesperson. Suspecting that the teacher was stuck in a career mismatch, the principal and Janet discussed her comfort level with the performance aspect of teaching. Janet

realized that she was putting all her energy into a career that required being "center stage" everyday—a situation she hated. The principal arranged a visit with a consultant for career exploration. Janet discovered a new career—one in which she could use her talents and find success.

SUMMARY

Burnout occurs when teachers feel insignificant. They feel there is no payoff in terms of accomplishment, recognition, or appreciation for their hard work. When teachers feel valued as individuals and a vital part of an important enterprise, their motivation, effort, and performance increase. Their schools are likely to achieve extraordinary results (Winter & Sweeney, 1994).

Principals can counteract burnout by (a) examining how teachers perceive the school environment and (b) reshaping their own behavior as well as factors within the school environment. Principals may consider assessing the school and their own behavior using the questions found in Table 5 (see Resources).

Tending the Flames

Supervision

A stitch in time saves nine.

SUPERVISION IS THE KEY

The first book on supervision was published in 1875. Written by William H. Payne, Professor of Science and the Art of Teaching at the University of Michigan, it was titled *School Supervision* (Blumberg, 1986).

Supervision is defined as the actions that enable teachers to improve instruction for students. Supervision ensures that teachers are both held responsible for satisfactory performance and at the same time engaged in professional growth and classroom-based assistance. It allows them to open their hearts, souls, and minds to another, thinking critically and actively planning improvements to their teaching (Glickman, 1990).

The introduction of supervision of instruction as an additional administrative task led to the gradual elimination of the teaching component of the principalship (Grady, 1990). Blumberg's (1986) history of supervision includes comments that represent early attitudes toward the importance of supervision, such as "As is supervision so will be the schools" and "the life-giving energy of a general supervision." Early supervisors appeared to have a great deal of faith in the desire of teachers to be better if they could be shown better ways to do things—"The inventive genius of our teachers is becoming aroused, and they are, very cautiously, however, venturing to leave the rotary [learning by rote] track of their predecessors" (Blumberg, 1986, p. 345). Another early supervisor said, "Some of our old teachers, who imagined themselves masters of their trade, have recently found out their mistake. One remarked to me, 'I have kept school a great many winters but now I am going to see if I can *teach* school'" (Blumberg, 1986, p. 268).

Payne (1875) described how a supervisor should help a teacher:

> THE ASSISTANCE WHICH SHOULD BE RENDERED TO TEACHERS—Whenever it is seen that a teacher is making a radical mistake which will compromise her success, a full and frank statement of the fact is required, and such helps should be given as the case seems to demand. No false delicacy should tempt one to withhold a candid opinion as to the nature and consequences of glaring faults. Otherwise, when disaster has come, and the teacher has forfeited her place, there is just ground for charging the superintendent with neglect of duty; for it is plain that skillful supervision ought to diminish the chances of failure. The superintendent ought to be a teacher of teachers, competent to detect the probable causes of failure, and able to suggest means which may avert disaster. This course is of special importance in the case of inexperienced teachers, whom judicious criticism and skillful assistance may save from undeserved failure. (Blumberg, 1986, p. 14)

A contemporary supervision problem is the hesitancy of administrators to be open and forthright about what they perceive to be shoddy teaching (Blumberg, 1986, pp. 15–16). The problems of supervision in the schools and the ways in which these problems are conceived and talked about have a long history. In a very real way, any of the problems that persist today in the field of supervision are not dissimilar from those dealt with in the past: (a) what we are about admits of no generalized solutions; and (b) there may be a sort of joyful mystery to our work, which, while sometimes frustrating, also provides a challenge to our wits and our skills in a way that makes life interesting (Blumberg, 1986, pp. 29–30).

Loneliness

Although schools are bustling places filled with students, teachers, and administrators, for the adults who work in them they may be incredibly lonely places. Principals find that they are prevented from discussing the burdens and challenges of their work with the other adults in the buildings because they have supervisory responsibilities for those other adults. The principal is in a very lonely role—described as the "loneliness at the top." Teachers are also lonely. Teachers do have peers in that there are other teachers in the school, but because of the organization of schools and the configuration of the work schedule, teachers have few opportunities to work with or have conversations with other teachers. Teacher isolation occurs in the "one teacher, one room" school structure and in the "one teacher, one class of students" configuration.

Supervision can help reduce the loneliness experienced by teachers. According to Glickman (1990), "The role of supervision is to change the attitude of many schools that a classroom is an island unto itself to an attitude that faculty is engaged in a common school-wide instructional task that transcends any one classroom—a cause beyond oneself" (p. 428). In the context of teacher burnout, we propose that supervision be construed as principals' being "present and available" to teachers in the schools. We are concerned with the very presence of supervision—how much *time* does the principal spend with individual teachers engaged in discussion of the goals of the teaching enterprise?

Supervise. Contrary to what some principals believe, teachers value supervision that helps them develop abilities and improve their teaching. One teacher described a situation in which many teachers were experiencing burnout and a principal who did not engage in any supervision.

> No teacher observations have been done. We need teacher observations, and someone to follow up on goals, do some benchmarking…some positive reinforcement. [We need some good one-on-one with the principal].

The "one-size-fits-all" traditional style of supervision is of dubious value, especially for teachers who are experiencing difficulty. As one principal said:

I don't find out anything from staged visits that I didn't already know from walking through the halls and in and out of classrooms everyday.

The first step in providing productive supervision is to let teachers know: (a) the type of supervision to expect, (b) the intended process and procedures, and (c) a timeline. Teachers feel less threatened when being evaluated by a supervisor who tells them what to expect and when to expect it (Richardson & Sistrunk, 1988).

Careful hiring is central to the supervision process. Teachers hired should have talents and skills that match the school and the students' needs.

Teacher supervision programs need to be designed to span teachers' careers, beginning with developmental induction programs for first-year teachers (Brock & Grady, 1997). As teachers gain experience, individualized supervision is tailored to their developmental levels, abilities, learning styles, and needs.

All teachers may benefit from involvement in peer coaching activities. The experience provides opportunities for new ideas, encourages sharing and interaction among colleagues, and decreases the loneliness intrinsic to teaching (Sergiovanni, 1995).

Plateauing

As principals undertake their supervisory work, they should consider the status of teachers in the schools. Milstein (1989) described the concept of plateauing in the teaching profession. He wrote that teachers "are in a 'front loaded' occupation (Lortie, 1975); i.e., we obtain professional privileges and advantageous working conditions when we first come into the profession, but these privileges and conditions are not likely to improve noticeably over time" (pp. 1–2). There are three forms of plateauing: (a) *structural*, which occurs when promotions are viewed as unobtainable; (b) *content*, which occurs when there is a sense that there is little or no challenge left in one's job; and (c) *life*, which represents an overall sense of routine and sameness about all aspects of life. Teachers have the potential for plateauing because they have been in well-defined positions for many years, are older, and work in mature organizations. Milstein (1989) reported that:

Twice as many teachers and administrators view themselves as structurally plateaued (47%) as do those considering themselves to be content plateaued (23%). Overall, teachers feel structurally plateaued more extensively than do administrators (58% to 34%). Education, as a relatively-flat hierarchical system, offers few promotion opportunities for administrators, but for teachers the problem is even greater. The front loaded career syndrome noted earlier is confirmed—*once tenured, there is usually no career ladder to climb within teaching!* (p. 9)

The Supervisor Is the Key

As the recognition of burnout spreads, teachers, administrators, and researchers seek ways of reducing the strain that is endemic to teaching. Empirical research suggests that the supervisor may be a key factor in the amelioration of stress and burnout (Cherniss, 1980). Principals may be both the source and the solution to burnout. Lawrenson and McKinnon (1982) found that special education teachers believed that 'hassles' with administrators were a leading cause of resignations. Several other studies found that lack of support on the part of supervisors and administrators was one of the strongest and most frequently cited sources of stress, low morale, and attrition in special educators (Johnson, Gold, & Vickers, 1982; McKnab & Mehring, 1984; Thomas, 1984; Zabel & Zabel, 1982). Fimian (1986) found that special education teachers who reported not receiving supervisory support also reported stronger and more frequent work-related stress (Cherniss, 1988, p. 449).

Richardson and Sistrunk (1990) reported that one common source of stress was the supervisory behavior of the principal. Metz (1980) found that major sources of professional burnout included administrative incompetence, bureaucratization, lack of administrative support, and lack of positive feedback. Litt and Turk (1986) included supervisory evaluation as an aspect of job tension in a study that also included lack of participation in decision making, concern for teachers' problems, and interest in professional development; these variables proved to be significant and were considered to be contributors to teachers' distress and dissatisfaction.

Maturity Level

The maturity of the follower is an important dimension of the leadership framework described by Hershey and Blanchard (1982). The needs and experiences of the teachers suggest the leadership or supervisory behavior to be used by a principal. Glickman (1990) described developmental supervision as a means of identifying teachers at different experiential stages.

Research on reading effectiveness shows the merits of different supervisory orientations when matched to the particular characteristics of the teaching staff. Reading effectiveness occurred in previous failure-prone schools and classrooms when teachers with little experience, competency, or desire to improve their instruction were monitored, evaluated and directed by the supervisor (principal) to use a new, systematic reading program (Vanezky, 1982). The results speak clearly for a directive orientation when the teaching force is unskilled and unmotivated. In still other schools, which had had several years of successful reading improvement, researchers noted frequent group problem-solving meetings and mutual adaptation of the curriculum (Humphries, 1981; McLaughlin & Marsh, 1978). For a staff that has successfully developed competency and motivation, a collaborative approach to future improvement appears to be in order. Finally, a staff with extensive background, competency, and motivation, who know how to work both together and alone, should find ways to improve student performance informally and independently. A nondirective orientation is most appropriate here. (p. 93)

Directive supervisors are skilled at accomplishing tasks, at getting and maintaining involvement, and at interacting with persons without exploiting them (Cribbin, 1981). Collaborative supervisors exhibit behaviors in which communication is freer and more authentic and in which participative decision making is the norm (Cribbin, 1981). Nondirective supervisors are essentially uninvolved, allowing teachers to make their own decisions (Richardson & Sistrunk, 1988). In Richardson and Sistrunk's study (1988), teachers perceived high levels of emotional exhaustion and depersonalization when they perceived collaborative supervisory behaviors. Teachers perceived lower levels of emotional exhaustion when they perceived nondirective supervisory behaviors. This indicates their preference to choose staff development activities personally, rather than collaborating with principals to develop plans or working under plans designed and directed by principals.

Consideration and Initiating Structure

Research on supervision in the workplace provides some clues about the types of actual behavior that might be associated with lower levels of burnout in special education programs. Two general dimensions typically have emerged: consideration and initiating structure (Schriescheim & Kerr, 1974). Supervisors who score high on consideration are sensitive, sympathetic, tolerant, and supportive. Supervisors high in structure are task oriented, maintain high standards, and help subordinates to perform better by providing clear goals and frequent feedback. Cook (1983) found that supervisor consideration, but not initiating structure, was significantly negatively correlated with burnout (Cherniss, 1988, p. 450).

Cherniss (1988) found in a study of two principals that the principal in a moderate-burnout school interacted with others significantly more than did the low-burnout school principal. The low-burnout principal interacted significantly more frequently with other administrators (primarily the principal's own supervisor in the central office). The low-burnout principal also interacted significantly more frequently with clerical staff. The differences in supervisory behavior were statistically significant: The low-burnout principal made statements significantly more often than did the moderate-burnout principal and listened to others significantly less often. The low-burnout principal engaged in significantly more support than did the moderate-burnout principal. The low-burnout principal observed others performing their jobs significantly less. The low-burnout principal spent significantly more time in the office and significantly less time in the staff lounge, in classrooms, and in halls. The findings of this exploratory study by Cherniss suggest that supervisors might help reduce staff burnout by spending more time in planning, organizing, and advocating for staff. Furthermore, a supervisor who listens more and talks less and who tries to engage in much "small talk" with staff will not necessarily be more supportive. On the other hand, the low-burnout principal in this study did spend more time discussing the significant work-related problems and concerns of her staff and made more of an effort to keep staff informed about critically important personnel matters, such as impending layoffs, salary raises, fringe benefits, and promotions (p. 454).

As principals examine their supervisory practices, they should consider the following questions: How much time is spent with teachers in a supervisory capacity? Is the time spent primarily in response to a crisis? Is the principal's time equally apportioned among all teachers?

Teachers need assistance with many different issues. Glickman (1990) recommends that an established procedure for meeting these needs be established. The procedure should be based on accessibility, arranged time, and delegation. Help must be available and accessible. A principal should:

> take the time to pause and speak with a certain number of teachers each day to ensure that by the end of the week every teacher has had the opportunity to bring up classroom concerns. Often such a brief exchange will alert the supervisor to a teacher's concern that should be followed up with a scheduled conference. (p. 292)

The principal should also be able to delegate teacher concerns to appropriate specialists who can offer more specific assistance with curricular or instructional concerns.

Principal's Leadership

The principal's leadership is clearly a factor in effective schools (Grady, Wayson, & Zirkel, 1989). Much has been written about principal leadership (Chance & Grady, 1990; Grady & LeSourd, 1989; LeSourd & Grady, 1988, 1989, 1991). All of the research on successful schools has cited a particular type of social organization, which Edmonds (1979) referred to as a "climate of expectation." Brookover and Lezotte (1979) called it "teacher belief that students could learn and not being satisfied with less," and Goodlad (1984) cited it as "goal participation and agreement." Rutter, Maughan, Mortimore, Ouston, and Smith (1979) identified this social organization as a "concept of ethos...the well-nigh universal tendency for individuals in common circumstances to form social groups with their own rules, values and standards of behavior" (p. 184). Where ethos was developed around a clear educational purpose, an effective school emerged:

> It should be emphasized that the more successful schools were not unduly regimented. Rather, good morale and the routine of people working harmoniously together as part of an efficient system meant that both supervision and support were available to teachers in a way which was absent in less successful schools. (Rutter et al., 1979, p. 184)

Every major research study on successful schools has noted the organizational phenomenon of collective action, agreed-on purpose, and belief in attainment (Pratzner, 1984; Rosenholtz, 1985). On the other hand, every major research study on ineffective schools has noted an absence of such purpose. Effective schools do not happen by accident: Supervision is the force that shapes the organization into a productive unit.

Unless the individual needs of staff members are linked with collective school goals, a school cannot be successful. Successful schools are characterized by teachers who enjoy working with each other as they accomplish school tasks. In many schools teachers enjoy being with each other, but the task dimension is missing. A successful school balances both dimensions so that people enjoy each other's company when they are accomplishing school goals.

A study by Mazur and Lynch (1989) separated two factors: leadership and support. Leadership was treated as the decision-making aspect of consideration, and support was treated as an organizational aspect. The finding was that although leadership (either democratic or autocratic) was not a significant predictor of teacher burnout, support was.

The negligible correlation of leadership style with burnout lends support to Halpin's (1966) view of the leader's role. Halpin's position was that initiating structure (the ways of getting the task done and the actions themselves) was independent of consideration (friendship, warmth, rapport). Mazur and Lynch's (1989) study separated the support aspect, which Halpin termed *consideration*, from leadership style, treating it more appropriately as an organizational factor. The findings suggested that the principal's approach to making decisions and the decisions themselves were significantly less important than the organizational support factors. If a principal sought consensus from the faculty in decision making but was generally unsupportive in terms of the organization's expectations and treatment, teachers would be vulnerable to burnout. Leader behavior instruments that confound the two dimensions fail to recognize the primary role that organizational factors play.

Principal's Responsibilities

If supervision is to improve instruction, then it must be an active force that provides focus, structure, and time for matters of curriculum and instruction. Supervision is intended to reduce the norms of the one-room schoolhouse—isolation, psychological dilemma, routine, inverted beginner responsibilities, and lack of career stages—and increase the norms of public dialogue and action for the benefit of all students. If supervision is to improve instruction, it must reshape norms and beliefs about the work culture of schools, as in the following propositions:

- ◆ Proposition 1: Supervision cannot rely on the existing work environment of schools to stimulate instructional improvement. Since the work environments of schools are routinized, isolated, and psychologically tense, teachers become private and regulated in their work rather than open to improvement.

- ◆ Proposition 2: Supervisors cannot assume that teachers will be reflective, autonomous, and responsible for their own development. Change will not automatically occur if left solely to teacher initiative.

- ◆ Proposition 3: Supervisors who hold formal leadership roles will have to redefine their responsibilities—from controllers of teachers' instruction to involvers of teachers in decisions about school instruction. Since successful schools are communities of professional colleagues rather than hierarchies of power and status, formal supervisors will need to view teachers as worthy of making decisions about their work (Glickman, 1990, p. 39).

Principals need to build a school culture that reduces burnout. Activities that contribute to culture building can include the following:

+ Communication—speaking with staff members and providing recognition for successes or follow-up on specific problems
+ Team building—developing common work groups, showing concern and building morale
+ Problem resolution—resolving problems quickly

Principals need to provide

+ Role modeling—three important behaviors are (a) demonstrating interest in classroom activities, (b) providing high-visibility leadership, and (c) displaying knowledge of and interest in curriculum and instruction
+ Direct supervision—supervision should be a type of evaluation (Glickman, 1990, p. 81)

Supervisory practices should include the following features:

1. Procedures are clear and evaluation criteria are well defined.
2. There is clear, consistent evidence that the supervision and evaluation functions are used as key mechanisms to link school and district offices.
3. Supervision and evaluation act not only as linkage mechanisms in their own right but also provide a strong base for the development of other potential linkage functions, especially goal setting and curriculum alignment.
4. Evaluation relies heavily on outcome controls, especially the evaluation of student achievement (Glickman, 1990, p. 82).

Renewal

For teacher renewal to occur, principals must provide financial support and released time. Renewal must be linked to the evaluation process. Nontenured or probationary teachers should be able to apply for tuition assistance, reimbursement for conference expenses, and other professional support. Tenured or career teachers should receive an annual stipend that they can use for professional expenses. During the evaluation process, teachers should receive encouragement and financial assistance to become contributors to the profession (Glickman, 1990). Faculty meetings should highlight the accomplishments of staff members, such as election to offices in professional organizations, conference presentations, publications, and selection for scholarships or fellowships.

Individual teachers should choose a supervisory evaluation model that best fits a specific stage of professional growth. In a progressive model of supervision and evaluation, teachers may move from clinical supervision to a more collegial consultation model. New teachers, or teachers who need close direction, are supervised according to the clinical model, in which the teacher and supervisor work together all year to enhance instruction. The supervisor observes several classes, writes a series of observation reports, and prepares a summative end-of-the-year evaluation on each teacher's progress.

Mature or highly skilled teachers may move to collegial consultation in which teachers are trained to work in peer teams to offer support for each other's instructional improvement. Master teachers, or those who are ready to take charge of their own professional growth, may move to the self-directed supervisory model, in which teachers monitor their own progress and write their own summative, year-end evaluations. When teachers actively take part in directing their own professional growth, they feel positive about the process and results (Glickman, 1990, p. 81).

A "Best" Case

Possibly the best discussion of a case of teacher burnout and the recovery process was told by an individual who recovered. Beverly Bimes, a National Teacher of the Year, offered the following advice:

> The first step toward teacher renewal is to help teachers get in touch with themselves by increasing their self-knowledge and freeing themselves from their psychological bondage. In attempting to live up to the teacher myth that a person

must give his or her entire life to be a dedicated teacher (as personified by the old-fashioned teacher image—no marital life, no social life), teachers find that they are caught in a type of psychological bondage.

After teachers become reacquainted with themselves, it is easier for them to look at their management of time, since inability to structure time produces stress. Over the years, they become locked into patterns of behavior that are not productive to learning or to them.

Many times teachers become so blocked by routine patterns that their work becomes mundane, and they lose sight of educational goals. One way to encourage teachers to broaden their perspectives, by seeing new alternatives, is through a peer visitation program. By visiting colleagues' classes, teachers have a great deal to gain.

Continuous opportunities for professional growth must exist in the form of meaningful inservice workshops. Released time for professional growth must be provided. With encouragement and with attention, teachers will remain in the classrooms where they belong. The key is helping teachers to get in control of their lives. (Bimes, 1981, pp. 3–6)

There are increasing numbers of teachers and schools that have established autonomous, collective, and intellectually challenging work environments. Those schools whose staff members knowingly combat the inertia of their profession and environment are most successful. In the most successful schools, supervision works to break up the routine, lack of career stages, and isolation of teaching and to promote intelligent, autonomous, and collective reason in order to shape a purposeful and productive body of professionals achieving common goals for students (Glickman, 1990, p. 40).

SUMMARY

Principals who "fight fires" have little opportunity to engage in the ongoing, goal-oriented teaching and learning conversation that keeps a school community on the focused path to excellence in teaching and student learning. The day of the principal can be fragmented. The principal's responsibility is to focus on the supervisory activities that support teachers in their work with students. If time spent with teachers is limited and focused only on crises, the teacher's lonely work will begin to contribute to burnout. Principals have a duty of care to teachers in their supervisory role. If principals are not present for teachers, then the outcomes will clearly lead to the destructive impact of burnout.

Fuel for the Flame

Staff Development as Prevention

Look forward to the Butterfly instead of stepping on the Caterpillar.

—Eleanor Wynne

THE IMPORTANCE

To be alive is to change. Human beings have the potential to grow intellectually throughout their entire lifetime. Adults, like children, need creative and intellectual stimulation in order to develop their full potential. Healthy individuals seek opportunities to develop. Those who do not are destined for stagnation and boredom. As one principal said, "Teachers who are burned out, negative, or disgruntled have stopped learning."

Preservice teacher education does not prepare a teacher for a lifetime career. The completion of teacher preparation and the first year of teaching are the beginning of what should become a career-long development process. In the words of one principal:

The first school I went to I asked, "What have you done to update skills?" Most of them hadn't done anything past their B.A. degrees. They told me, "We're poor, we're harried, we're busy"…that's breeding ground for people being disgruntled. Left alone, some teachers become candidates for burnout.

Each year of teaching should bring new knowledge, develop new skill, and provide creative and intellectual stimulation. One principal explained:

> Every year you work you have to get better. If experience is worth anything it should be because you're getting better at what you do. I think that's the key to keeping a staff growing. Those people, who never want to get involved, they're not growing and if they're not growing they're a liability.

Through staff development activities, teachers can improve their knowledge and skills, thus enhancing their sense of efficacy and morale. The benefits include increased competence, confidence, and self-esteem and the feeling that they are fulfilling their potential. Teachers are more satisfied with themselves, their work, and others (Andrew, Parks, & Nelson, 1985).

The Principal's Role

The principal's role in staff development is encouraging and assisting teachers to fully develop the talents and skills that will enhance their teaching and improve student learning. As one principal noted:

> We're not as successful as we want to be so we need to keep trying different things. If we keep plugging away at the same methods, we're probably going to keep getting the same results. What could we do differently?

The faculty in a typical school includes a wide variety of ages, career stages, educational backgrounds, and developmental levels. The principal's challenge is to provide opportunities that motivate and energize according to individual needs.

Origins of Staff Development

Throughout the 1960s and 1970s the focus of inservice programs was to update teachers in subject areas, teaching skill, and improving their ability to work with students. In the 1980s, the focus broadened to include personal growth as well as professional growth. Self-awareness and personal growth were recognized as essential to change and professional growth (Casteel & Matthews, 1984).

Current State of Staff Development

The inservice of past decades no longer meets current developmental needs. The words of a discouraged principal describe a frequent scene in schools—teachers bored and inattentive during a staff development session.

A few teachers in the front row were actually listening, or perhaps pretending to listen. The rest were dozing, correcting papers, or whispering to their neighbors—like teenagers. I was embarrassed and furious. The time and money I wasted on this session.

Often staff development programs consist of "one-shot"sessions on curricular issues or new teaching methods. Sustained improvements seldom occur as a result of these sessions. Most teachers view them as a waste of time, providing nothing of substance relevant to their daily tasks. Many teachers deem traditional staff development to be ineffective (Karst, 1987).

A tacit assumption is that teachers are not capable of determining their own needs for professional growth. Instead, the principal's role is to assess teacher effectiveness and recommend changes for overall professional improvement. Teachers are seldom afforded the chance to reflect on and determine their own development needs.

Teachers who continue their professional development have usually found avenues to do so outside of the normal inservice and staff development programs provided by their school district. Teachers who are not so resilient and self-directed find little meaningful assistance or direction (Karst, 1987).

Effective staff development has a broader base than the traditional forms of inservice and graduate classes. Teachers are instead viewed as professionals who are capable of directing their own professional growth. Staff development strategies encourage teachers to reflect on their teaching as well as to learn from collegial interactions.

Contemporary development activities include professional dialogue with colleagues, collaborative curriculum development, peer supervision, peer coaching, and action research. Opportunities for teachers to interact and learn from one another are key to professional development (Monahan, 1996). Some school districts encourage teachers to develop portfolios or strive for National Teacher Certification as well as to write for publication.

The Funding Issue

Principals and school districts often struggle to obtain funding for staff development. Although public opinion polls support professional development for teachers, many districts do not provide compensation and time during the school year for teacher development (Recruiting New Teachers, 1998). In spite of this, many creative principals find ways to encourage professional growth.

The Relationship of Burnout to Staff Development

Teacher burnout is the antithesis of professional growth. Individuals suffering burnout are characterized by negativity and despair and are resistant and unable to adapt to change. They are unable to grow professionally because their personal development is at a standstill.

Burnout should be a concern of administrators as they prepare staff development plans. Information about burnout may prevent the derailing of careers. Teachers who are aware of the sources and symptoms of burnout as well as coping strategies and preventative measures may be able to avoid the malady (Casteel & Matthews, 1984).

The Substance of Development

One component of ongoing staff development should focus on teachers' ability to maintain a good balance between their work and personal lives. Asking teachers to leave personal lives at home is not possible. Teachers who have acquired self-awareness, confidence, and adaptability to change are more likely to embrace new ideas and change in their professional lives.

Programs that offer the following topics may be effective in reducing the potential for burnout.

- Cognitive restructuring
- Time management
- Physical wellness
- Social skill development
- Classroom management
- Spiritual renewal

Although these are not substitutes for administrative changes in the workplace, they may assist teachers in developing habits and skills that reduce the likelihood of burnout.

Cognitive Restructuring. Cognitive restructuring is used to assist an individual in viewing situations from new perspectives. It involves examining interactions between events and beliefs to determine reasons for reactions and responses. At the core of cognitive restructuring is distorted thinking, which results in negative interpretations of events. When the reaction is determined to be unwarranted or negative, the individual considers alternative ways to view the situation and subsequently the emotional response.

The following are examples of distorted thinking according to McKay, Davis, and Fanning, as cited in Casteel and Matthews (1984, pp. 12–13):

- Filtering—focusing on negatives while filtering out positive aspects
- Polarized thinking—viewing situations as black or white
- Overgeneralization—basing conclusions on incidental information
- Mind reading—assuming knowledge of others' thoughts and feelings
- Catastrophizing—overreacting to the imagined worst possible scenario
- Personalization—assuming the response of others as directed to you

+ Control fallacies—considering yourself either wholly responsible or the victim of fate
+ Fallacy of fairness—viewing your opinion as fair and not understanding disagreement
+ Blaming—placing blame on someone or yourself for every event
+ Should—having your own personal view of how you and others should act
+ Emotional reasoning—believing all reasons are true
+ Fallacy of change—believing that you can change others if you try
+ Global labeling—forming opinions by generalizing qualities
+ Being right—viewing your opinions as right and different views as challenges
+ Heaven's reward fallacy—naively expecting rewards for all your efforts

Time Management

My unhappiness was the unhappiness of a person who could not say no.

—Dazai Osamu

A heavy workload is inherent to the teaching profession. Teachers may benefit from instruction in time-management skills (Starnaman & Miller, 1992).

Time management provides new ideas about organizing time efficiently and eradicating time wasters. Everyone has the same amount of time. Yet some individuals accomplish enormous amounts of work without becoming overcome by stress. Their secret is efficient use of time.

Steps in time management include time analysis, goal setting, prioritization, delegation, and action.

1. Analysis: During the analysis phase, the individual selects a period of time and records all activities. The analysis period might cover every hour for a week or 2 weeks to establish patterns. Data are analyzed and categorized to see how time is actually spent.

2. Goal setting: Determine long- and short-term goals for a designated period of time, such as 1 year. The goals should be realistic and measurable.

3. Prioritization: Rank the goals according to their importance using categories such as "urgent and essential," "can be delayed but essential," and "desirable but not urgent." Learn to say "no" to people and actions that do not lead to goal accomplishment.

4. Delegation: Delegating nonessential tasks to someone else can create additional time. Delegating work to paraprofessionals, volunteers, and secretaries provides teachers with more time for instructional preparation and interacting with students.

5. Action: Goals are more readily accomplished when broken into smaller increments. Action plans with timelines established for completion of each activity will facilitate accomplishment of the later goals.

Physical Wellness. Proper diet and rest are obviously essential to maintaining good physical and mental health. However, busy teachers often neglect their nutrition and feel they do not have time for adequate sleep. Staff development sessions that address nutrition and rest may be beneficial for some teachers.

Exercise is recognized as essential to a healthy lifestyle and is an effective stress reducer. Teachers who plan time for regular exercise find that in addition to the obvious physical benefits, tension is reduced and they have more energy. Some schools encourage exercise by inviting personnel to use the gymnasium, track, and weight room at the end of the day. Another option is offering an exercise class or organized sports for school personnel. Schools without adequate space or equipment may be able to collaborate with a nearby school or community center.

Mental diversion can also dissipate tension. Any non-school-related activity that occupies one's thoughts in a pleasurable way could combat negativity. Activities involving music, art, gardening, reading, woodworking, and stamp or antique collecting are a few common examples. The nature of these activities is limited only by the creativity of the individual. Although these may not be included in staff development sessions, encouraging teachers to engage in individual, non-work-related pursuits is important. Some teachers need to be taught that "it's OK" to relax, laugh, and have fun.

Relaxation training demonstrates the importance of the connection between mind and body and teaches the individual how to elicit relaxation responses at will (Casteel & Matthews, 1984). Staff development sessions that show teachers varying methods of relaxation may be beneficial.

Social Skills. Problems with people factor heavily in the burnout process. Many teachers report that student discipline and problems with parents are causes of burnout. Yet some other teachers easily establish rapport and gain the support of students and parents. They appear to have a personality that engages students and endears them to parents. Although the difference is usually attributed to innate personality traits, their success is more likely due to acquired social skills. They have learned how to work with students and parents.

Principals can provide staff development sessions that address the acquisition of interpersonal and communication skills, such as (a) the teachers' classroom behavior, (b) reflective listening, and (c) conflict resolution. An initial session might focus on the behavior of teachers who are known for achieving positive rapport with students. Nichols (1991) reported that teachers who are effective exhibit the following behaviors: they smile, look at students when they talk to them, and exchange everyday pleasantries. In classrooms where teachers have discipline problems, these behaviors are noticeably absent.

These behaviors may not have been taught during teacher preparation. In their zeal to have well-behaved students, teachers may in reality be provoking inappropriate behaviors. One principal reflected on how this truth was revealed to her.

I was homeroom teacher for a group of junior high students who had notorious discipline problems. The first few months I was stern and enforced strict rules. I became exhausted, while they continued to behave with no improvement.

In desperation I tried a new approach—smiling and greeting each one by name in the morning. During the day I spoke to each one about a nonschool topic—music, sneakers, something they liked. I slipped treats, notes, jokes, and books in individual desks for birthdays, to congratulate a success, or when I found something that one of them would enjoy. I tried to establish a personal relationship—to connect—with each of them.

It worked and I learned a valuable lesson. While they didn't receive school-wide awards for model behavior, in my classroom they behaved and learned. We became a team...I moved with them to the next grade, remaining their teacher for two enjoyable years.

Another seemingly simple yet often overlooked interpersonal skill is listening. Although taught to children, some teachers forget to practice it: Stop what you are doing, look at the person, think about what they say, ask questions to be sure you understand. Simple to recite, challenging in practice, and essential for rapport with people of any age.

Teachers need to actively listen when students speak to them, giving the same attention they would to an adult. This is the first rule of respect.

Listening is a critical factor in enhancing and maintaining teachers' relations with parents. Parents have information, opinions, and feelings that need to be shared. When teachers do not listen, parents feel that their information and feelings are not valued. Teachers who actively listen to both students and parents can avoid many stress-producing situations.

Conflict is an inevitable, yet stress-provoking, facet of life. Disputes between students, confrontations with parents, and disagreements between colleagues occur. The conflict itself is neither inherently good nor bad. However, the outcome of the conflict may be either positive or negative, depending on how it is handled. Teachers who know how to negotiate and resolve a conflict will experience less stress and will be able to turn a potentially destructive situation into a productive and positive conclusion.

Classroom Management. Teachers who have continuing discipline problems are at a higher risk for stress and burnout. In spite of having effective interpersonal skills, some teachers have difficulty with the group dynamics that evolve in the classroom. Providing assistance in classroom-management skills may be indicated for a teacher who experiences ongoing problems with students (Starnaman & Miller, 1992).

Spiritual Renewal. The spiritual dimension encompasses the values and beliefs that inspire and provide direction to our lives. Renewal in this area is critical to the individual's sense of peace and purpose. Individuals who have a sense of direction and purpose and who are at peace with themselves are able to withstand the stresses of daily life (Covey, 1989).

Spiritual renewal is an essential component of a staff development program. Renewal may take the form of prayer, meditation, reading, listening to music, or enjoying the beauty and serenity of nature.

Some principals encourage spiritual renewal by having retreat days held in a quiet setting away from the school. A typical retreat begins with an inspirational presentation and time for discussion, followed by quiet time alone to reflect.

Teachers view spiritual renewal as essential and a primary means of preventing burnout. One teacher reflected on the value of spiritual renewal:

My first principal provided wonderful staff development. She focused on both our personal growth as well as professional growth. She initiated me into teaching and helped me develop as a teacher. It was a good, formative experience. She also did a lot of personal growth things for us...she had a real mission to keep us all going in the right direction as far as spiritual growth.

She made sure we had one or two retreats a year...at the beginning of the year we had a retreat away from the school. We discussed the school goals and our own personal and professional goals. Writing down my goals, having a mission, helped give me a sense of where I was going. She gave us personal affirmations. She had an open door to her office. Everybody was always in her office telling her about his or her day. She was a good listener and very supportive. She had a way about her...a genuine concern for us.

THE DEVELOPMENT PROCESS

The greatest good you can do for another is not just share your riches, but reveal to them their own.

—Disraeli

Staff development may take a variety of forms, depending on the context of the school environment and the needs of the teachers. A comprehensive development program begins with a teacher induction program for first-year teachers and continues throughout teachers' professional careers.

First-Year Teacher Induction

An effective entry into professional development is through a first-year teacher induction program that includes a mentoring component. The purpose of the induction program is to prepare beginning teachers for the transition from the university to the reality of classroom teaching. Induction programs are a means to acquaint new teachers with the school culture and to assist them in analyzing and handling problems commonly encountered. The support from the principal, their mentor, and colleagues is essential in eliminating feelings of discouragement and burnout (Brock & Grady, 1997).

Induction programs can decrease the possibility of problems leading to burnout by including sessions on stress factors in teaching. Identifying factors that cause personal stress as well as appropriate responses may diminish discouragement when stress occurs.

Continued opportunities to discuss problems decrease feelings of isolation while providing possible solutions and support.

Mentoring

Mentoring is often as beneficial to the mentor as it is to the novice teacher. The process of mentoring requires the analysis and justification of one's teaching methods. The process of collaborating and sharing ideas can be a renewing experience for the mentor teacher. As one principal explained:

This year I have a program with a university in which their education students are working with our students. My teachers act as mentors. They've had to reexamine what they do and how they do it. The results are remarkable. My teachers have become energized...one of them hadn't done anything for years! It's just good for everybody.

Replacing Isolation With Collegiality

Individual development plans are important, yet those that are most successful involve collaboration and dialogue with other teachers. Shared visits between colleagues, team teaching, and exchange programs with other schools are valued experiences. Other districts use collaborative curriculum development, peer supervision, peer coaching, and action research to provide opportunities for teachers to interact and learn from one another (Monahan, 1996; Nichols, 1991; Ryerson, 1981).

Career Ladders

To dispel the lack of career stages for teachers, some educators propose the development of career ladders by creating levels of teacher status based on skill rather than tenure, encouraging lateral moves between grades and subjects, and developing a master teacher/mentor system (Ryerson, 1981).

Sabbatical

Others suggest the necessity for time away from school to provide renewal. Leaves of absence, paid or unpaid, provide a break for teachers to refresh themselves, try another career, take time with their family, or recover physically and emotionally. A study by Gaziel (1995) reported that a sabbatical year that included a training program had a positive effect on teachers' professional identity, reduced burnout, and increased desire to remain in the profession.

SUMMARY

Keating (1993) used a garden metaphor in describing the significance of the supervisor-worker relationship. The application of her "garden lessons" is fundamental to successful staff development for teachers.

> When I invite a plant into my garden, I assume responsibility for that plant, since I have made decisions crucial to the plant's well being. When I devote the appropriate caring and attention to my plants, they usually thrive. When I do not, they wither or even die...I realized that there was a direct relationship between how much attention I devoted to the plant and how well that plant did. (p. 63)

Kerpen (1993) suggested a new paradigm for the workplace that has relevance for teacher morale and schools. In her new paradigm, "people are treated as the most valuable asset and their concerns and well-being are given top priority" (p. 73). When that paradigm becomes reality, teachers will develop professionally in an atmosphere of support and confidence, classroom performance will be enhanced, and school improvement will occur.

Stoking the Fire

Improving the Workplace

I never did a day's work in life. It was all fun.

—Thomas A. Edison

IF IT AIN'T BROKE

Drivers who fail to maintain their vehicles are usually shocked and bewildered when their cars stop working. Likewise, school administrators who fail to maintain teacher morale are similarly shocked and bewildered when burnout problems erupt in their schools. Their common response is, "But everything seemed OK."

Burnout is alive, fueled by the reactionary stance of many schools. Although viewed by the uninformed as a rare event, the malady is common and costly to people and to school organizations. Treating burnout and repairing the damage to people and schools is more difficult and costly than preventing it (Maslach & Leiter, 1997).

A Proactive Approach

The prudent approach is to establish measures to prevent burnout before it occurs. Schools with engaged and happy teachers are not random occurrences. They have administrators who create working conditions in which teachers feel both personally and

96

professionally valued and rewarded. Their success is the result of careful planning to ensure smooth operations in the context of a wholesome working environment. It is based on determining the operational and environmental conditions that will make teachers most productive and satisfied with their work. The benefit to schools is a staff of loyal, hardworking, and dedicated teachers who provide long-term service to the school and profession. Symptoms of burnout are avoided.

A Committed Administration

The success of any efforts to decrease teacher stress relies on the commitment of the school's administration. Farsighted school administrators are dedicated to creating schools where teachers are happy and engaged in their teaching. Burnout prevention is critical because principals know that happy teachers are essential to student learning and to the success of their schools.

Operation and Environment

Fundamental to the well-being of teachers is a well-organized and functioning school with a culturally healthy environment. Well-developed policies and procedures minimize teacher stress and provide a mechanism for responding to inevitable conflicts in organizational life (Maslach & Leiter, 1997). The school's culture should model values that support school goals while ensuring a healthy working environment for teachers.

Although a well-organized and smoothly operating school is a prerequisite to teacher engagement, it does not preclude the existence of stressful environmental conditions. The external appearance of order may actually mask an internal environment that is unhealthy and full of stress. The "emperor has no clothes" syndrome is a human response. Busy administrators believe what they want to be true and are shocked when they learn otherwise.

Planning to Prevent Burnout

Each school needs to establish a plan to assess, identify, and reduce areas of stress. The school's administration has the pivotal role in creating the prevention plan. Principals can and should take measures to prevent burnout, both by assessing the stress level of teachers and by taking corrective action before signs of burnout are evident. Steps include analysis, planning, implementation, and evaluation. One teacher suggested:

> Survey what teachers are thinking. If you see trends, prioritize them, select the top three [issues], and start working on them. Have a chart to measure how things change. Don't expect overnight success, but have a systematic way of [intervening] and making things change.

Step 1—Assessment and analysis. School stress can be eliminated or reduced by identifying potential sources and assessing associated levels of teachers' stress. The initial task is to gather baseline data on the level of teacher satisfaction and dissatisfaction.

The responsibility for assessing environmental stress and initiating constructive change lies with the school's administration. In addition, teachers should be asked to help identify the source of the problem and provide input on how to reduce or resolve it (Capel, 1992). Use of multiple strategies and inclusion of many individuals will provide more complete and accurate information. Data sources might include

- Surveys of teachers
- Focus groups
- Teacher exit interviews
- Conversations with individuals
- Feedback from parents and students
- Observations

Table 5 (see Resources) is a sample teacher survey for school assessment and self-assessment.

An observant principal can readily detect early signs of stressful conditions. The following behaviors are among those that indicate teacher stress and the likelihood of a stress-producing situation in the organization. The underlying causes for these behaviors will be target areas for assessment.

+ Frequent absenteeism

+ High teacher turnover

+ Lack of school pride

+ Grumbling and complaining

+ Poor relationships among teachers

+ Unhappy parents

+ Student discipline problems

+ Lack of support for school policies

+ Lack of productivity

+ Resistance to change

+ Rumors

+ Poor attendance at school functions

+ Unhappiness with the administration

Step 2—Planning for Change. Once data are gathered and analyzed, stressful conditions can be targeted. The next step is planning for organizational change according to the data analysis. If teachers were involved in the assessment, they need to be informed of the findings and included in planning for changes. If the plan involves opportunities for employee activities, such as social events and fitness programs, participation needs to be voluntary.

The plan needs to be simple and realistic, and it must include a timeline, cost, and process for implementation. Teacher input is necessary in planning for implementation. Plans that are unrealistic, too expansive, or too costly may never be implemented. When change does not occur, teachers become resentful and disillusioned. Instead of preventing a problem, an unwary principal may "pour water on smoldering coals."

Step 3—Implementing Change. Implementation of the plan needs to occur according to the established timeline. However, one should not expect enthusiasm or even cooperation with regard to the change. Organizational change, even when desirable to teachers, takes time. Teachers need to become comfortable and trusting of the change.

Faculty may not respond with confidence and enthusiasm. The principal may become discouraged. Yet discarding the plan without ample time for acceptance would be a mistake. Successful change requires time, patience, and persistence.

Step 4—Evaluating Progress. An ongoing process for evaluation of teacher stress and success of current measures is essential. Changes implemented after the initial assessment should be reviewed to determine their effectiveness. Periodically, a thorough reassessment of teacher stress needs to be accomplished (Cedoline, 1982).

LIKELY TARGETS FOR DISTRESS REDUCTION

What areas should principals target to prevent burnout? Maslach and Leiter (1997) suggested that the following areas of organizational life are key factors in preventing burnout: values, workload, control, reward, community, and fairness. Capel (1992) suggested investigating organizational and administrative issues, physical environment, and personnel relationships. Other researchers suggested reviewing the following leadership variables: vision, goals, expectations, support, stimulation, modeling, culture, and school structure (Leithwood, Menzies, Jantzi, & Leithwood, 1996).

Teachers experiencing burnout suggested the following areas for analysis: vision and values, hiring, community, culture, collegiality, autonomy, workload, discipline, parents, support, communications, recognition, voice, safety, resources, compensation, and staff development. The significance of each of these areas will be discussed in the following sections.

Vision

Schools without burnout have teachers and administrators who share a common vision for the school and who are dedicated to achieving that vision. Together they develop a mission statement and goals that drive their actions toward that vision.

The vision for each school is determined by the needs of the population served. Regardless of school setting, teachers and administrators need to be guided by a shared vision of common goals (Chance & Grady, 1990; Grady & LeSourd, 1989; LeSourd & Grady, 1988, 1989, 1991).

When teachers feel part of an important effort and know the importance of their role, the potential for burnout decreases. The likelihood of loyalty and dedication increases. When the values of teachers and administrators differ, the vision cannot be shared. Burnout is sure to follow. An experienced and once dedicated teacher said:

> My school was part of a reorganization; two communities joined two school faculties and two groups of students in one building. I was in favor…thought it was a progressive move. The board of education brought in all new administration.
>
> However, the new philosophical base became radically different than before… very different than mine. I had ownership and had been a dedicated part of my school, putting in extra time for minimal monetary reward. But…I believed in what I was doing. The new [standards and curriculum] negated all I had worked for and believed in. [The school] lost academic rigor and expectations…I talked with the principal and we disagreed philosophically. He wouldn't change…I decided that I didn't belong anymore. I went to the board and asked to be released from my contract.

Hiring

The importance of shared values makes the hiring and induction of new teachers critical. The interview process should include questions that determine if the candidate's educational philosophy and core values match those of the school. For instance, one should ask specific questions of the candidate about parent-teacher relations and then ask similar questions when checking references at the previous workplace (Townley et al., 1991). By doing so, the interviewer determines whether or not the candidate is a match for the school. The interviewer should likewise provide information about the school so that the candidate has a clear picture of requirements and expectations. The interview thus becomes the initial step in the induction process.

Community

Relationships between colleagues and administration either discourage or encourage teacher burnout. One teacher described the lack of community in her school:

We called the cafeteria and faculty lounge snake pits. Teachers made fun of students, parents, and each other. Even the principal joined in, making caustic comments about some of the teachers. I hated to be in there…but was afraid to leave for fear that I would be the next target.

To maintain momentum and establish a strong community, some principals schedule annual retreat days for faculty to revisit and discuss the school's vision and mission. Central to the retreat are discussions about how the written mission is carried out by individual actions. The purpose is to translate the mission from a lifeless piece of paper into a living reality. Teachers understand more concretely their individual and collective importance in fulfilling the mission. Additionally, faculty become better acquainted and gain increased respect for differing opinions. An element of fun and good humor are key ingredients to the retreat's success.

Culture

A healthy school culture promotes a sense of community and augments a teacher's sense of professionalism (Friedman, as cited in Vandenberghe & Huberman, 1999). Some schools have cultures that appear positive on the surface but that may support behaviors that are stress provoking and that precipitate burnout. For example, a school culture that supports a strong work ethic is desirable. However, if the work ethic becomes unbalanced and teachers' lives become so devoted to school that they neglect their personal lives, the culture becomes destructive.

A culture that is predicated on an expectation that all teachers arrive long before school begins, stay late every night, participate on many committees, and take home stacks of work may be setting the stage for burnout. Although a strong work ethic and dedicated teachers are important aspects of a healthy school culture, an excessive focus on "work" creates more problems than it solves. A beginning teacher reported:

The other teachers raise their eyebrows and look knowingly at each other when I arrive just before or leave right at the contracted time. They make me feel as though I am not dedicated enough, but I have a baby that I need to take care of at home. I feel guilty when I leave and guilty when I stay.

Teachers in a culturally healthy school understand and value relaxation, play, socialization, and time with family and friends.

Collegiality

Teachers need support from others who share the same daily classroom stresses. Unfortunately, the organization of school schedules usually precludes teacher interaction.

Arranging opportunities for more social interactions could provide teachers with the support needed to deal with the inherent stressors in their daily work (Starnaman & Miller, 1992).

Autonomy

Among the most annoying problems faced by teachers is being told what or what not to teach and being subjected to petty interruptions during their classes. When curricula and teaching methods are programmed and predetermined, teachers are denied the autonomy to exert instructional leadership (Sergiovanni, 1995). Teachers treated in this manner become insecure about their status as teaching professionals and cynical toward the system. Wise principals guard against infringements on teachers' rights to teach within the limits of defined school policies and do not permit routine interruption of classes (Gallagher, Bagin, & Kindred, 1997).

Workload

Quantitative. Since workload is a factor in burnout, principals need to know the extent of the quantitative workload for each faculty member, as well as the individual's ability to handle it. Every attempt needs to be made to keep workload as equitable as possible and to avoid assigning additional duties, especially those that conflict with classroom assignments, to an already overworked teacher (Starnaman & Miller, 1992). Relief of the burden or reducing the hours of teaching and providing some free time for planning or reflecting, especially for those who have difficult classes, will decrease the likelihood of burnout (Capel, 1992; Huberman, 1993). One principal, who inherited a school with a destructive work ethic, reported encouraging teachers to go home after school and discouraging working in classrooms on weekends. The teachers needed permission to change.

Qualitative. Satisfaction from one's work is a powerful motivator and an important reward. Teachers who are presented a challenge for which they have the prerequisite skills generally meet the challenge with enjoyment and satisfaction. However, when teachers have skills that are greater than the challenge requires, they become bored. By contrast, when faced with a challenge for which they are unprepared, teachers become anxious (Sergiovanni, 1995). The risk for burnout increases when teachers' work leaves them bored, anxious, or frustrated. In other words, finding the right balance between level of skill and challenge is critical.

One factor in boredom is teachers' frequent role as caregiver or supervisor. Ask teachers why they burn out and they often identify their role as "babysitter" as the reason. Teachers perceive the many hours devoted to supervising students outside the classroom as time better spent planning and preparing for teaching.

Reassignment is a way to qualitatively change teachers' workloads. School reassignments should not be viewed as negative but rather as an opportunity for professional growth and new challenges. A systematic schedule for teacher reassignment within school districts or within schools can provide new vigor for teachers.

Discipline

Chronic problems with student behavior are factors in teacher burnout. Skills in classroom management and interpersonal relationships are critical to a teacher's success. Students want teachers who relate to them as individuals with warmth and friendliness. Teachers, too, enjoy close relationships with students and are gratified by their expressions of warmth (Friedman, as cited in Vandenberghe & Huberman, 1999).

When these skills are absent, teachers struggle with student discipline. Teachers regard good discipline as essential to effective learning. When student discipline becomes a continual problem, teachers doubt their own ability to teach and manage their classrooms.

Although they want to improve the situation, they are unable to regain what they perceive as satisfactory learning conditions. Unless they are provided with some relief from the disruptive class or assisted to improve their discipline practices, burnout is almost certain. Principals, observing teachers struggling with discipline, need to assess the situation and determine a course of action to alleviate the problem (Brock & Grady, 1997). Principals must provide instruction in classroom management and strategies for working with difficult students to all faculty (Starnaman & Miller, 1992).

Parents as Partners

A healthier learning environment exists for both teachers and students when parents are active partners in the teaching process. Raising parents' awareness of school issues and teaching objectives encourages cooperation with teachers. Principals have an important role in promoting parental involvement, making parents aware of conditions in which teachers work, and encouraging respect for teachers (Friedman, as cited in Vandenberghe & Huberman, 1999).

Parents who are nonresponsive or combative increase the stress experienced in the classroom. Principals can provide relief by interceding and assisting teachers in resolving persistent issues with parents. Teachers may also benefit from instruction in conflict negotiation and resolution.

Support

Support from the principal is instrumental in reducing role conflict and role ambiguity. Teachers who have frequent positive contacts and who have established rapport with the principal report less role stress and have increased satisfaction with their work (Starnaman & Miller, 1992).

Actions Speak Louder Than Words. Administrators whose behavior is incongruent with what they say will have difficulty relating to teachers. Teachers believe what they see the principals do, rather than what principals say. For instance, the principal who reports the need for budget cuts while lavishly redecorating the administrative offices destroys the credibility and sincerity of the message and damages teacher-principal relations. Although redecorating may not have infringed on or had any relationship to the instructional budgets, the teachers do not have that information. Their perception is the disregard of the principal for instructional materials to do their job (Gallagher et al., 1997).

Differing perspectives create conflict. School administrators tend to communicate with a value perspective that is different than that of teachers. What the principal believes is important to the teachers may not be true. When this occurs, the good intentions of the principal are misinterpreted and misunderstandings occur. Relations improve when principals attempt to understand teachers' needs and communicate from their perspective.

Communications

Communications can be improved by establishing a structured communications program in the school that includes orientation for new teachers, one-on-one conversations, opportunities for two-way feedback, and internal publications. Teacher morale suffers when teachers learn about happenings in the school and district from outside sources or receive erroneous messages from within. Principals should be sensitive to the need of teachers to be kept informed of activities and issues affecting the school. Institutions can respond to this need by distributing a school employee newsletter written in a simple format. Some schools report success with a daily (or weekly) bulletin. This provides a simple, inexpensive way for all school employees to know what is happening. The addition of humorous stories, recognitions, thank-yous, and personal news promotes high morale and esprit de corps (Gallagher et al., 1997).

All schools should provide handbooks clearly stating the district's and school's general policies and procedures. Particularly troublesome for teachers are instances in which schools do not have clearly stated policies and procedures regarding student discipline.

In addition to a formal communications program, teachers want personal conversations with the principal. They want the principal to pay attention to them, to listen to their concerns and issues, and to provide affirmation and counsel (Brock & Grady, 1997). These conversations enable the principal to learn the values and priorities of the teachers and enable the teacher to learn what the principal views as significant for the school (Gallagher et al., 1997). The rapport established is critical to the prevention of burnout. In addition, regular meetings with individuals provide opportunities for principals to address early symptoms of burnout.

Recognition

A critical form of communication from the principal is recognition. All individuals like to be recognized for a job well done and to know that their efforts are appreciated. Recognition is as simple as a note, letter, or phone call that thanks, praises, or congratulates. Yet busy principals, although they know the importance of recognition, frequently fail to deliver it (Gallagher et al., 1997).

Voice

Teachers should be included in discussions and decisions regarding proposed curricular and organizational changes. This strategy reduces teacher uncertainty and provides awareness and understanding of impending change, thereby reducing stress (Capel, 1992; Starnaman & Miller, 1992).

Teachers who have a voice in the decisions of the school feel a sense of ownership. Administrators who subscribe to this democratic decision-making process speak of the importance of relationships and interconnectedness among all school personnel.

Safety

Teachers are assaulted at alarming rates. Although no consistent national figures are available, studies show that in 1996 approximately 11% of the more than 2.5 million U.S. teachers had been victims of violence in and around schools. Other studies reported that 5,200 teachers were attacked monthly. Teachers cannot be expected to teach effectively when they are in physical danger. In some situations, the emotional distress is so great that teachers are filing suits against students (Reske, 1996).

In some schools, teachers feel that they are being denied a duty of care. Many are demanding workplace safety as an issue in contract negotiations. Teachers are asking that school boards be legally bound by contract to adopt policies designating schools as safe havens, to carry out risk assessments, and to ensure that safety precautions are taken, including necessary installations of security equipment. Others are calling for special insurance policies for injuries that might be sustained from violent attacks at school, with special packages relating to stress disorders and teacher burnout. Bonus pay for teachers working in high-risk schools is an emerging trend (Black-Branch & Lamont, 1997).

Resources

Adequate facilities and resources are fundamental to performing one's job and are prerequisites for success. Yet, some teachers struggle to obtain adequate materials and textbooks for their students. Others have inadequate facilities, furniture, and space to perform their work. When performance is impeded in this manner, disillusionment is sure to follow. Principals can eliminate the burnout that results when teachers lack resources by ensuring that teachers have adequate resources to effectively perform their jobs (Gallagher et al., 1997).

Compensation

An adequate salary is necessary for teachers to live a balanced life. "Moonlighting" to supplement a teaching income should not be a necessity for those in the teaching profession (Tishler & Ernest, 1989). Administrators should make every effort to support increases in teachers' salaries. When compensation is not treated as a legitimate need, teachers feel disillusioned. Reasonable compensation is essential to maintaining high morale and productivity (Cedoline, 1982).

Staff Development

Staff development programs established to benefit teachers tell them that the administration views them as important. A program that helps teachers improve professionally is one that provides direction and opportunities, such as attendance at conferences and workshops, reimbursements for courses taken, and salary increments for professional development.

All teachers new to a school or the profession deserve a well-structured orientation program that includes assignment to a mentor. Their success is dependent upon proper familiarization with the school and the principal's expectations (Brock & Grady, 1997; Gallagher et al., 1997).

SUMMARY

Burnout should not be considered endemic to the teaching profession. Many schools are populated with happy, engaged, and productive teachers. However, sources exist at the individual, institutional, professional, and societal levels that can compromise and endanger career satisfaction. Although some of the factors in burnout are beyond the control of a principal, many of the organizational causes can be addressed. A prudent approach to burnout is taking steps to prevent it before it occurs.

Principals who opt for prevention are dedicated to operating schools in which teachers feel personally and professionally valued. They are keenly aware that happy and engaged teachers are essential to student learning and to the long-term success of their schools.

They take measures to prevent burnout by assessing the stress level of teachers and taking corrective action before signs of burnout are evident. Steps include analysis, planning, implementation, and evaluation.

For any change to be fully implemented, lasting, and effective, the change must directly improve classroom teaching conditions for teachers. Farber (as cited in Vandenberghe & Huberman, 1999) said it best: "If where teachers spend most of their time—the classroom—remains fundamentally unaltered (or too dramatically altered) and fundamentally unrewarding, then other changes, as well intentioned as they may be, are not likely to have an enduring effect on a teacher's vulnerability to stress and burnout" (p. 160).

Unless workplace conditions are favorable to teachers and teaching, the conditions for productive learning will not exist for students. As expensive as burnout is in terms of teacher attrition, absenteeism, and use of medical benefits, how do we measure the cost of poor teaching? The low productivity brought about by teacher burnout is not quantifiable but is clearly recognizable in the miseducation of our youth.

There are no easy answers or "quick fixes" for burnout. Solutions do exist when principals are willing to invest the time and energy to discover them. The solutions include creating happier and more productive environments for teachers and students. Those who persist will decrease teacher burnout and be richly rewarded by increased student learning.

Resources

TABLE 1 Symptoms of Burnout

Physical	Intellectual	Emotional	Social	Spiritual
Chronic fatigue/ Exhaustion	Information overload	Overwhelmed by demands	Rude	Threatened by others' needs
Physical ailments	Poor concentration	Anxious, tense, nervous	Avoids interactions	Breakdown in personal values
Frequent accidents	Lack of alertness	Irritable, impatient, angry	Avoids social gatherings	Desires change
Avoidance of eye or physical contact	Can't meet deadlines	Alienated, cynical, withdrawn	No time for others	Desires escape from situation
Alcohol, drug, food, misuse	Lacks creativity	Not in control	Irritable or impatient	Despair

TABLE 2 Burnout Inventory

Item	SA	A	N	D	SD
I feel overwhelmed with work					
I feel that I have no control over my work					
I feel angry at the students					
I feel frustrated with parents					
I feel angry at the administration					
I feel exhausted at work					
I have lost interest in teaching					
I avoid interacting with the other faculty					
I seldom interact with students					
I avoid meeting with parents					
I am irritable toward students					
I dread coming to work					
I can't wait to leave at the end of the day					
I feel unappreciated by parents					
I feel unappreciated by the administration					
I have problems with student discipline					
I have problems getting along with parents					
I feel teachers have little public respect					
I feel teachers are not treated as professionals					

TABLE 2 - Continued

I have no time for a personal life					
I take work home with me					
I feel compelled to arrive early and stay late at work					
I have input into school decisions					
I like the grade or subject that I teach					
I feel proud to be a teacher					
I feel respected by the community					
I enjoy interacting with students					
I find time to collaborate with colleagues at work					
I enjoy teaching					
I would like to teach a different grade or subject					
I would like to transfer to another school					
I would like to quit working altogether					
I would quit teaching if I could find another job					
I never really wanted to be a teacher					
I feel trapped in my job					
I loved teaching when I started but I have lost my enthusiasm					
My lessons are not well prepared					
My teaching is a source of pride for me					

TABLE 2 - Continued

Item	SA	A	N	D	SD
My principal is willing to listen to my concerns					
I am comfortable sharing my concerns with the principal					
I feel that people would think less of me if I asked for help					
My principal treats me with respect					
I am well informed about school events and issues					
I feel exhausted					
I need help in my classroom					
My workload is too great at school					
I am overwhelmed with work at home					
I struggle with family problems					
My health interferes with my work					
Lately I have been absent from work					
Lately I have felt ill					
I feel sad and depressed					
I enjoy my work					
I look forward to coming to school					
I feel rewarded by my students' success					
I always wanted to be a teacher and I still feel that way					

TABLE 2 - Continued

	SA	A	N	D	SD
I would rather teach than have a job that paid a higher salary					
The atmosphere in my school is congenial					
The parents in my school are supportive					
We have good staff development opportunities at my school					
We have well-behaved students					
Morale is high in our school					
My principal is attentive to teachers' concerns					
We have opportunities for spiritual and personal growth at school					
I have adequate resources for my teaching					
My school is clean and well maintained					
We have a sense of community in our school					
I feel inadequate as a teacher					
I perform responsibilities that parents should					
Public criticism of teachers bothers me					
I worry about violence occurring in my school					
I worry about my safety in school					

NOTE: Teachers are asked to indicate agreement with the items using the scale SA = Strongly Agree; A = Agree; N = Neither Agree nor Disagree; D = Disagree; SD = Strongly Disagree.

TABLE 3 Satisfying Working Conditions

Physical	*Intellectual*	*Emotional*	*Social*	*Spiritual*
Personal safety	Autonomy in choices	Financial security	Affiliation	Sense of personal worth
Secure belongings	Intellectual stimulation	Job security	Acceptance	Worthwhile work
Adequate resources	Creative opportunities	Achievable workload	Collaboration	A cause beyond oneself
Climate-controlled building	Professional growth	Respect/ Appreciation	Fun/ Laughter	Satisfaction with work
Clean/ Well-maintained building	Challenging work	Sense of achievement/ Success	Time for family	Satisfaction in personal life

TABLE 4 Principal's School Assessment and Self-Assessment
Respond Yes, No, or Don't Know to the Following Questions

Do the teachers in my school feel that they	Yes	No	Don't Know
Make a contribution			
Have a sense of self-direction			
Belong to something			
Are part of something important			
Know where they fit in			
Are competent/successful in one area			
Can act independently			
May select options or alternatives			
Have valued opinions			
Have choices			
Are cared for as individuals			

Do teachers have	Yes	No	Don't Know
Adequate resources			
A clean building			
An orderly environment			
Personal safety			
Collegiality			
Time to teach			
Time for planning			

Do I	Yes	No	Don't Know
Focus on individuals			
Look for strengths			
Place teachers in settings appropriate for their talents			
Allow mistakes			
Value input			
Listen			

TABLE 4 - Continued

Do I	Yes	No	Don't Know
Assist teachers to maximize their potential			
Support their decisions			
Make teachers feel good about themselves			
Encourage new ideas			
Provide recognition			

Am I	Yes	No	Don't Know
Cheerful			
Optimistic			
Respectful			
Honest			
Trustworthy			
Reliable			
Decisive			
Fair			
Helpful			
Knowledgeable			
Current			
Participatory			
Welcoming			
Open			
Flexible			
Adaptable			
Expert			
Collaborative			
Accessible			
Encouraging			
Creative			
Enthusiastic			

TABLE 5 Teacher's School Assessment and Self-Assessment

I would like your help in improving our school. Your confidential and anonymous responses to this survey will provide valuable information about how we might make our school an even better place for teachers to work and students to learn.

A summary of all responses will be prepared, and together we will be able to develop plans based on the responses.

Item	*SA*	*A*	*N*	*D*	*SD*
I believe that the quality of my teaching has a definite impact on the success of my school					
I understand how I contribute to the school's mission					
As a faculty, we regularly review our progress toward school goals					
The school district's vision provides a clear direction for the future					
The faculty is guided by a sense of the school's shared vision and values					
My school welcomes parent involvement in children's learning					
My school listens to parents' concerns					
My school makes student learning a top priority					
Our school responds quickly and appropriately to parental feedback					

Item	SA	A	N	D	SD
All teachers understand the school's policies and procedures					
I have the resources (materials and equipment) to do quality teaching					
My workload does not affect the quality of my teaching					
I am encouraged to actively participate in solving school problems					
Teachers communicate openly in the school					
I receive the information I need regarding school affairs and activities					
Our administrator does a good job of communicating school decisions					
I have trust in the information that I receive from school administrators					
I have the freedom I need to use my own judgment in teaching					
We practice teamwork in our school					
There is good cooperation between teachers in the school					
Orientation and induction for new teachers is effective					
I benefited from the assistance of a mentor during my first year					

My present assignment provides an opportunity to develop my talents					
My principal encourages me to develop my teaching ability					
I know what is expected of me regarding my teaching performance					
I receive adequate feedback on my performance					
I have recently received praise for good work					
My performance is measured against clearly defined expectations					
My school uses a fair evaluation system					
My school celebrates its successes					
My school recognizes teacher success and achievements					
My school recognizes student achievement and successes					
I feel that I have opportunities to develop professionally at my school					
I am compensated fairly for my work					
Compared with other schools, my salary is competitive					
I am satisfied with the benefits provided by my school					

TABLE 5 - Continued

Item	SA	A	N	D	SD
Information about school and district benefits is clearly communicated					
My principal treats me with respect					
My principal responds to my requests for assistance					
My principal values my ideas					
My principal encourages me to do high-quality teaching					
My principal will stand up for me					
My principal cares about me as a person					
My principal follows through on commitments					
My principal treats all personnel fairly					
We have fun while getting the job done					
I have made friendships at school					
I am able to adjust work hours when needed to meet personal needs					
My principal recognizes the importance of my personal life					
My principal takes an interest in the well-being of the staff					

I like teaching at this school					
The physical working conditions at my school are good					
I believe that policies are administered fairly					
I am satisfied with my job					
My present assignment provides opportunities to use my talents and skills					
The morale in the school is good					
I am proud to work at my school					
I am optimistic about the future success of this school					
I can achieve my career goals while working at this school					
I would encourage my friends to teach at this school					
I plan to teach at this school for many years					

NOTE: Teachers are asked to indicate agreement with the items using the scale SA = Strongly Agree; A = Agree; N = Neither Agree nor Disagree; D = Disagree; SD = Strongly Disagree.

Figure 1. Factors in Teacher Burnout

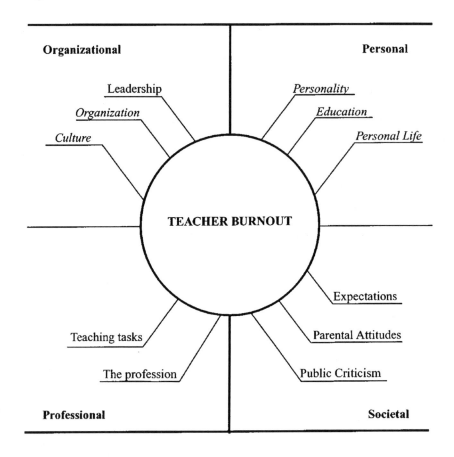

Figure 2. Continuum of Organizational Health

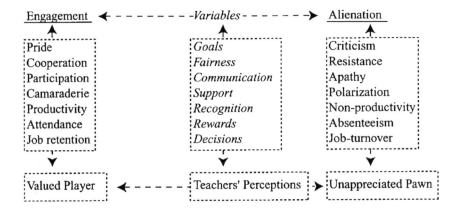

References

Andrew, L. D., Parks, D. J., & Nelson, L. A. (1985). *Administrator's handbook for improving faculty morale.* Bloomington, IN: Phi Delta Kappa.

Barrentine, P. (Ed.). (1993). *When the canary stops singing.* San Francisco: Berrett-Koehler.

Bimes, B. J. (1981, April). *Dealing with teacher stress and burnout.* Paper presented at the Annual Meeting of the National School Boards Association, Dallas, TX.

Black-Branch, J. L., & Lamont, W. (1997). Entrenching contractual clauses for safety in the educational workplace into the collective agreement: The new frontier in employment law. *Collective Negotiations, 26,* 125–135.

Blase, J., & Kirby, P. C. (1992). The power of praise—Strategy for effective principals. *NASSP Bulletin, 76*(528), 69–77.

Blumberg, A. (1986, April). *The language of supervision: Perspectives over time.* Paper presented at the Annual Meeting of the American Educational Research Association, San Francisco, CA.

Brock, B. L. (1999). Perceptions of teacher burnout in Catholic schools. *Catholic Education: A Journal of Inquiry and Practice, 2,* 281–293.

Brock, B. L., & Grady, M. L. (1995). *Principals in transition: Tips for surviving succession.* Thousand Oaks, CA: Corwin.

Brock, B. L., & Grady, M. L. (1997). *From first-year to first-rate: Principals guiding beginning teachers*. Thousand Oaks, CA: Corwin.

Brock, B. L., Nelson, L., Grady, M. L., & Losh, M. A. (1998). Public schools and law enforcement agencies: Joining forces for school safety. *Connections, 1*, 21–26.

Brock, B. L., & Ponec, D. L. (1998). Principals and counselors: Creating effective elementary school counseling programs. *Educational Considerations, 26*(2), 33–37.

Brookover, W., & Lezotte, L. W. (1979). *Changes in school characteristics coincident with changes in student achievement*. East Lansing: Michigan State University, College of Urban Development.

Byrne, B. M. (1992, April). *Investigating causal links to burnout for elementary, intermediate, and secondary teachers*. A paper presented at the Annual Meeting of the American Educational Research Association, San Francisco, CA.

Cadavit, V., & Lunenburg, F. C. (1991, April). *Locus of control, pupil control ideology, and dimensions of teacher burnout*. Paper presented at a meeting of the American Educational Research Association, Chicago, IL.

Capel, S. A. (1992). Stress and burnout in teachers. *European Journal of Teacher Education, 15*, 197–211.

Casteel, J. F., & Matthews, D. B. (1984, November). *Burnout prevention programs: A must for staff development*. Paper presented at the national conference of the National Council of States on In-service Education, Orlando, FL.

Cedoline, A. J. (1982). *Job burnout in public education: Symptoms, causes, and survival skills*. New York: Teachers College Press.

Chance, E. W., & Grady, M. L. (1990). A model for developing visionary leadership. *NASSP Bulletin, 74*(529), 12–18.

Cherniss, C. (1980). *Professional burnout in human service organizations*. New York: Praeger.

Cherniss, C. (1988). Observed supervisory behavior and teacher burnout in special education. *Exceptional Children, 54*, 449–454.

Cook, K. E. (1983). *The relationship between teacher perceptions of supervisory behavioral style and perceived teacher burnout*. Unpublished doctoral dissertation, University of Connecticut, Storrs.

Covey, S. R. (1989). *The seven habits of highly effective people*. New York: Simon & Schuster.

Cribbin, J. J. (1981). *Leadership: Strategies for organizational effectiveness*. New York: Amacom.

Dworkin, A. G. (1987). *Teacher burnout in the public schools: Structural causes and consequences for children.* Albany: State University of New York Press.

Edmonds, R. R. (1979). Effective schools for the urban poor. *Educational Leadership, 37,* 15–24.

Farber, B. A. (1982). Stress and burnout in suburban teachers. *Journal of Educational Research, 77,* 325–331.

Farber, B. A. (1991, April). *Tracing a phenomenon: Teacher burnout and the teacher critics of the 1960s.* Paper presented at the Annual Meeting of the American Educational Research Association, Chicago, IL.

Fimian, M. J. (1986). Social support and occupational stress in special education. *Exceptional Children, 52,* 436–442.

Frataccia, E. B., & Hennington, I. (1982, February). *Satisfaction of hygiene and motivation needs of teachers who resigned from teaching.* Paper presented at the Annual Conference of the Southwest Educational Research Association, Austin, TX.

Freedman, S. F. (1991). *Small victories.* New York: Harper & Row.

Friedman, I. A. (1991). High- and low-burnout schools: School culture aspects of teacher burnout. *Journal of Educational Research, 84,* 325–333.

Friedman, I. A. (1995). Student behavior patterns contributing to teacher burnout. *Journal of Educational Research, 88,* 281–289.

Friesen, D., Prokop, D. M., & Sarros, J. C. (1988). Why teachers burn out. *Education Research Quarterly, 12*(3), 9–19.

Gallagher, D. R., Bagin, D., & Kindred, L. W. (1997). *The school and community relations* (6th ed.). Boston: Allyn & Bacon.

Gaziel, H. H. (1995). Sabbatical leave, job burnout and turnover intentions among teachers. *International Journal of Lifelong Education, 14,* 331–335.

Glickman, C. D. (1990). *Supervision of instruction: A developmental approach* (2nd ed.). Needham Heights, MA: Allyn & Bacon.

Goodlad, J. I. (1984). *A place called school.* New York: McGraw-Hill.

Gottfredson, G. D., & Gottfredson, D. C. (1985). *Victimization in schools.* New York: Plenum Press.

Grady, M. L. (1990). The teaching principal. *Research in Rural Education, 6*(3), 49–52.

Grady, M. L., Bendezu, M. A., & Brock, B. L. (1996). Principals' perceptions of school safety. *Leadership Nebraska, 6,* 18–20.

Grady, M. L., Krumm, B. L., & Losh, M. A. (1997). The state department of education's role in creating safe schools. In A. P. Goldstein &

J. C. Conoley (Eds.), *School violence intervention: A practical handbook* (pp. 58–71). New York: Guilford Press.

Grady, M. L., & LeSourd, S. J. (1989). Principals' attitudes toward visionary leadership. *The High School Journal, 73*(2), 103–110.

Grady, M. L., Wayson, W. W., & Zirkel, P. A. (1989). *A review of effective schools research as it relates to effective principals* (UCEA Monograph Series). Tempe, AZ: University Council for Educational Administration.

Halpin, A. W. (1966). *Theory and research in administration.* New York: Macmillan.

Hershey, P., & Blanchard, K. H. (1982). *Management of organizational behavior: Utilizing human resources* (4th ed.). Englewood Cliffs, NJ: Prentice Hall.

Herzberg, F., Mausner, B., & Snyderman, B. (1959). *The motivation to work.* New York: Wiley.

Hewitt, P. B. (1993, November). *Effects of non-instructional variables on attrition rate of beginning teachers: A literature review.* Paper presented at the Annual Meeting of the Mid-South Educational Research Association, New Orleans, LA.

Hips, E. S., & Halpin, G. (1991, November). *Job stress, stress related to performance-based accreditation, locus of control, age, and gender as related to job satisfaction and burnout in teachers and principals.* Paper presented at the Annual Meeting of the Mid-South Educational Research Association, Lexington, KY.

Hoy, W. K., & Miskel, C. G. (1991). *Educational administration: Theory, research, and practice.* New York: McGraw-Hill.

Huberman, M. (1993). Burnout in teaching careers. *European Education, 25*(3), 47–69.

Humphries, J. D. (1981). *Factors affecting the impact of curriculum innovation classroom practice.* Unpublished doctoral dissertation, University of Georgia, Athens.

Johnson, A. B., Gold, V., & Vickers, L. L. (1982). Stress and teachers of the learning disabled, behavior disordered, and educable mentally retarded. *Psychology in the Schools, 19*, 552–557.

Karst, R. R. (1987, April). *New policy implications for inservice and professional development programs for the public schools.* Paper presented at the Annual Meeting of the American Educational Research Association, Washington, DC.

Keating, K. E. (1993). Organizational gardening: A metaphor for the new business paradigm. In P. Barrentine (Ed.), *When the canary stops singing* (pp. 50–70). San Francisco: Berrett-Koehler.

Kerpen, M. L. (1993). Balance: The ultimate challenge of the 21st century. In P. Barrentine (Ed.), *When the canary stops singing* (pp. 73–86). San Francisco: Berrett-Koehler.

Kijai, J., & Totten, D. L. (1995). Teacher burnout in the small Christian school: A national study. *Journal of Research on Christian Education, 4*, 195–218.

Lawrence, R. (1998). *School crime and juvenile justice.* New York: Oxford University Press.

Lawrenson, G. M., & McKinnon, A. J. (1982). A survey of classroom teachers of the emotionally disturbed: Attrition burnout factors. *Behavioral Disorders, 8*, 41–49.

Leithwood, K., Menzies, T., Jantzi, E., & Leithwood, J. (1996). School restructuring, transformational leadership and the amelioration of teacher burnout. *Anxiety, Stress, & Coping, 9*(3), 199–215.

LeSourd, S. J., & Grady, M. L. (1988). Principal leadership for instructional goal attainment. *Clearing House, 62*, 62–64.

LeSourd, S. J., & Grady, M. L. (1989). Visionary attributes in principals' description of their leadership. *The High School Journal, 73*, 111–117.

LeSourd, S. J., & Grady, M. L. (1991). What is a visionary principal? A research brief. *NASSP Bulletin, 75*(533), 107–110.

Litt, M. D., & Turk, D. C. (1986). Sources of stress and dissatisfaction in experienced high school teachers. *The Journal of Educational Research, 78*(3), 178–185.

Lortie, D. (1975). *Schoolteacher: A sociological study.* Chicago: University of Chicago Press.

Maslach, C. (1982). *Burnout—The cost of caring.* Englewood Cliffs, NJ: Prentice Hall.

Maslach, C., & Leiter, M. P. (1997). *The truth about burnout.* San Francisco: Jossey-Bass.

Mazur, P. J., & Lynch, M. D. (1989). Differential impact of administration, organizational, and personality factors on teacher burnout. *Teaching & Teacher Education, 5*, 337–353.

McGuire, J. (1993). Democracy in practice. *The Executive Educator, 15*(9), 28–29.

McKnab, P. A., & Mehring, T. A. (1984, April). *Attrition in special education: Rates and reasons.* Paper presented at the Annual Convention of The Council for Exceptional Children, Washington, DC.

McLaughlin, M. W., & Marsh, D. D. (1978). Staff development and school change. *Teacher College Record, 80*, 69–74.

Metz, P. K. (1980). An exploratory study of professional burnout and renewal among educators. *Dissertation Abstracts International, 40,* 4308A–4309A.

Milstein, M. M. (1989, March). *Plateauing as an occupational phenomenon among teachers and administrators.* Paper presented at the Annual Meeting of the American Educational Research Association, San Francisco, CA.

Monahan, T. C. (1996). Do contemporary incentives and rewards perpetuate outdated forms of professional development? *Journal of Staff Development, 18*(1), 44–47.

Nichols, P. (1991, May). *Through the classroom door: What teachers and students need* (Mountain Plains Information Bulletin). Des Moines, IA: Mountain Plains Regional Resource Center.

Payne, W. (1875). *School supervision.* Cincinnati, OH: American Book Company.

Potter, L. (1995, March). *How to improve teacher morale: Create a duty-free school.* (Available from the National Association of Secondary School Principals, 1904 Association Drive, Reston, VA 20191–1537)

Pratzner, F. C. (1984). Quality of school life: Foundations for improvement. *Educational Researcher, 13*(3), 20–25.

Recruiting New Teachers (1998). *The essential profession: A national survey of public attitudes towards teaching, educational opportunity and school reform.* Belmont, MA: Author.

Reinhold, B. B. (1996). *Toxic work.* New York: Dutton.

Reske, H. J. (1996, April). When detentions fail. *ABA Journal, 82,* 22–23.

Richardson, G. D., & Sistrunk, W. E. (1988, November). *The relationship between secondary teachers' perceived levels of burnout and their perceptions of their principals' supervisory behaviors.* Paper presented at the Annual Meeting of the Mid-South Educational Research Association, Louisville, KY.

Richardson, G. D., & Sistrunk, W. E. (1990, November). *Supervision, burnout, and evaluation of instruction.* Paper presented at the Annual Meeting of the Mid-South Educational Research Association, New Orleans, LA.

Rosenholtz, S. J. (1985). Effective schools: Interpreting the evidence. *American Journal of Education, 93,* 352–388.

Rutter, M., Maughan, B., Mortimore, P., Ouston, J., & Smith, A. (1979). *Fifteen thousand hours: Secondary schools and their effects on children.* New York: Random House.

Ryerson, D. (1981). Organizational strategies to reduce the risk. *Vocational Education, 56*(8), 40–41.

Sarros, A. N., & Sarros, J. C. (1990). How burned out are our teachers? A cross cultural study. *Australian Journal of Education, 34*, 145–152.

Schriescheim, C. A., & Kerr, S. (1974). Psychometric properties of the Ohio State leadership scales. *Psychological Bulletin, 81*, 756–765.

Sergiovanni, T. J. (1995). *The principalship* (3rd ed.). Needham Heights, MA: Allyn & Bacon.

Shipka, B. (1993). Corporate poverty: Lessons from refugee camps. In P. Barrentine (Ed.), *When the canary stops singing: Women's perspectives in transforming business* (pp. 89–103). San Francisco: Berrett-Koehler.

Starnaman, S. M., & Miller, K. I. (1992, January). A test of a causal model of communication and burnout in the teaching profession. *Communication Education, 41*, 41–53.

Stern, A., & Cox, J. (1993). Teacher burnout: The dull reality. *Music Educators Journal, 80*(3), 33–36, 49.

Thomas, W. R. (1984, April). *Occupational stress among exceptional education teachers.* Paper presented at the Annual Convention of The Council for Exceptional Children, Washington, DC.

Tishler, A. G., & Ernest, B. (1989, November). *Career dissatisfaction among Alabama teachers: A follow-up.* Paper presented at a meeting of the American Educational Research Association, Chicago, IL.

Townley, K. F., Thornburg, K. R., & Crompton, D. (1991). Burnout in teachers of young children. *Early Education and Development, 2*, 197–204.

Truch, S. (1990). *Teacher burnout and what to do about it.* Novato, CA: Academic Therapy Publications.

Vandenberghe, R., & Huberman, M. A. (Eds.). (1999). *Understanding and preventing teacher burnout: A source book of international research and practice.* Cambridge, UK: Cambridge University Press.

Vanezky, R. L. (1982, January). *Effective schools for reading instruction.* Address to the California (Calfee) Reading Project, Stanford University, Palo Alto, CA.

Winter, J. S., & Sweeney, J. (1994). Improving school climate: Administrators are key. *NASSP Bulletin, 78*(564), 65–69.

Zabel, R. H., & Zabel, M. K. (1982). Factors in burnout among teachers of exceptional children. *Exceptional Children, 49*, 261–263.

Index

**CORWIN
PRESS**

The Corwin Press logo—a raven striding across an open book—represents the happy union of courage and learning. We are a professional-level publisher of books and journals for K–12 educators, and we are committed to creating and providing resources that embody these qualities. Corwin's motto is "Success for All Learners."